Perfect Pairings

Perfect Pairings

more than 100 recipes with wine matches
for easy entertaining

photography by Peter Cassidy

LONDON • NEW YORK

Senior Designer Barbara Zuñiga
Editor Rebecca Woods
Production Gary Hayes
Art Director Leslie Harrington
Editorial Director Julia Charles

Indexer Hilary Bird

First published in 2012 by
Ryland Peters & Small
20–21 Jockey's Fields
London WC1R 4BW
and
Ryland Peters & Small, Inc.
519 Broadway, 5th Floor
New York NY10012
www.rylandpeters.com

10 9 8 7 6 5 4

ISBN: 978 1 84975 264 0

A catalogue record for this book
is available from the British Library.

A CIP record for this book is available
from the Library of Congress.

Printed and bound in China.

Notes

• All spoon measurements are level, unless otherwise stated.
• Eggs are medium unless otherwise specified. Uncooked
or partially cooked eggs should not be served to the very
old, frail, young children, pregnant women or those with
compromised immune systems.
• When a recipe calls for the grated zest of lemons or limes
or uses slices of fruit, buy unwaxed fruit and wash well
before using. If you can only find treated fruit, scrub well in
warm soapy water before using.
• Ovens should be preheated to the specifed temperature.
Recipes in this book were tested in a regular oven. If using
a fan-assisted oven, follow the manufacturer's instructions
for adjusting temperatures.

Contents

How Wine Can Enhance Your Enjoyment of Food

Food, wine and friends. Can there be a better formula for an evening's entertainment? No one element is as good in isolation. Friends without food or wine: good to see them, but it can all seem rather rushed. Food without wine or friends: functional rather than fun. Wine without food or friends simply isn't as enjoyable at all.

Countries where wine is a part of life, like France and Italy, know this instinctively. The wine goes on the table automatically – they know the food tastes better as a result. It helps relax your guests and aids digestion, helping you to savour each mouthful more intensely. Sipping wine slows down the pace of the meal.

It also – and this hasn't yet fully been recognized – helps the busy host or hostess make an impact with their entertaining. If you've bought a ready-made or takeaway meal (as so many of us do these days), your guests will more than likely be aware of that (after all, they do it too!). But if you choose an intriguing wine or other drink to serve with it – one that is not only interesting in its own right but heightens the flavour of the food – then you'll have created an experience to remember.

The beauty of this approach is that you don't have to be an experienced cook to pull it off. You simply need to develop a flair for what ingredients work well together, just as those who dress stylishly can put together a 'look', or others can make their house look great by the colours and furnishings they choose. Learn about wine in Making the Most of Every Glass (see pages 15–37), then dive into the menus and use the recipes and wine matching suggestions to create unforgettable feasts that are always accompanied by the perfect tipple.

This book is very much written with the pressures of modern life in mind. We all want to show our friends hospitality, but we simply don't have enough time in our busy days to make everything from scratch. So we need to be more imaginative and flexible about the way we do it.

Don't feel duty bound to offer a full meal. Of course, it's fun occasionally to throw a full-blown dinner party, such as the Fine Wine Dinner (see page 144), but it's equally enjoyable to just invite friends round for a few tapas (see page 122) or a cheese and wine night (see page 53). They'll love the novelty and, faced with far less work in the kitchen, so will you!

Why not try reflecting the seasons in your choice of food and drink? You'll make life easier for yourself and more enjoyable for your guests. Let local food growers and producers inspire you with the first of the new season's organic vegetables and throw together a Farmers' Market Dinner (see page 130). Towards the end of the year, make an old-fashioned Vegetarian Harvest Supper (see page 108) with the pick of the autumn's produce.

When the weather hots up, take your lead from those who live year-round in a tropical climate and serve spicy but cooling food (see page 88). Then, when temperatures hit zero, stay indoors and huddle up around the comforting sort of fare suggested in the Midwinter Supper (see page 94). Even the cheeseboards you serve your guests can be given an imaginative seasonal twist, as you'll see from the ideas on pages 48–50.

Use the menus and ideas in this book as a starting point for a new style of entertaining at home – one where the idea comes first, then you invite friends round to share the experience, rather than inviting them round then desperately wondering what to cook for them.

So cook if you feel like it, and buy in food if you don't. Use interesting and carefully chosen drinks – beers, cocktails, juices and liqueurs – as well as wine, to make your meals special and memorable. Most importantly, relax and enjoy!

Food and Wine Matching Made Easy

If you've ever tasted a food you love with a wine that matches it perfectly, you'll know that the combination of the two can be even better than the food or the wine on its own. But how best to find those perfect pairings? The old 'white wine with fish, red wine with meat' rule is a little dated, as anyone who has enjoyed a seared tuna steak with a Pinot Noir well knows. Wine has changed. Food has changed. The only rule now is that there are no hard and fast rules – just combinations that most people are likely to enjoy.

Basically, there's no great mystique about it. Simply use your existing knowledge of food and think of wine as another ingredient to take into account when you're planning a meal – rather as you would when you choose

a vegetable side dish, or a sauce to serve on the side. The more food and wine matches you try, the more confident you'll feel, so take every opportunity to try out different combinations, particularly in restaurants that serve a good variety of wines by the glass or suggest food and wine pairings with their menu. Here are some simple pointers that may help you:

- Always match the wine to the sauce, rather than the basic ingredient. Chicken, for example, can be cooked in any number of different ways, so it's more useful to think about whether it's served in a creamy, rich white wine and mushroom sauce (in which case, opt for a smooth, dry white), a red wine sauce like coq au vin (a similar wine to the one you used to cook it), a Thai green curry sauce (a fruity, off-dry white) or a barbecue sauce or marinade (a ripe, fruity red).

- Bear in mind the temperature and intensity of the dish that you are serving. Dishes that are served raw or delicate steamed dishes will need lighter wines (usually white) than ones that are roasted, seared or grilled (more often red). Homemade dishes will often be more intensely seasoned than bought ones, so may require more intensely flavoured wines to match them.
- Take into account what else is on the plate. Strongly flavoured vegetables such as asparagus, red cabbage or beet(root), or fruity or spicy salsas and relishes, can make a difference to the wine you choose. If you served grilled salmon with asparagus, for instance, you'd probably go for a Sauvignon Blanc, while if you made a spicy mango salsa to go with it, opt for a Semillion or Semillion-Chardonnay, or a light, fruity red.
- If you're planning to serve several different wines during the course of a meal, a good general rule of thumb is to start with the lighter, drier wines and then move on to the richer, more full-bodied ones. Usually, that means white wines followed by red, but you could easily serve a full-bodied white with a main course or a lighter red followed by a more full-bodied one.
- Dessert wines need to be sweeter than the food they're accompanying, otherwise they can taste sharp.
- Feeling unsure? Then try imagining wine as a fruit. If it's light and citrussy, it will go best with dishes where you might think of adding a squeeze of lemon, as you would to fish or chicken. Whereas a wine with ripe red berry fruit flavours will probably go best with ingredients to which you might think of adding red fruits, such as duck, turkey or lamb.

You can refer to the at-a-glance wine and food matching guide on the following pages to help you get started on creating your own successful pairings. And remember – the more you experiment, the more naturally perfect pairings will come to you. Happy eating…and drinking!

Matching Wine to Food

Finding a precise match for a dish can be tricky because there are so many variables: how it is cooked, whether there are any strong spice or herbal accents, how many other ingredients there are on the plate. To make it as easy as possible, this guide concentrates on the style of food rather than individual dishes, but giving specific examples where appropriate. If you can't find what you're looking for here, try an online guide, such as www.matchingfoodandwine.com.

Soups

You don't always need wine with a soup, as one liquid doesn't need another. The thicker the soup, the easier it is to match.

Thin soups e.g. consommés or spicy South-East Asian broths: are better without wine, although dry sherry will go with a traditional consommé.

Smooth creamy soups e.g. light vegetable soups: go for a smooth, dry, unoaked white such as Chablis or Soave.

Chunky soups: should be treated as a stew – they can take a medium-bodied white or a red such as a Côtes du Rhône.

Starters/appetizers

Given that they're served at the beginning of a meal, a crisp, dry white, aromatic white or rosé is generally most appropriate. Sometimes a light red can work too.

Cold, fish-based starters such as prawn/shrimp or crab salads or terrines: a crisp, dry white such as Sancerre or other Loire Sauvignon Blanc, or a Riesling (particularly good with smoked fish). Chablis is the classic match for oysters.

Hot, fish-based starters e.g fishcakes or scallops: Chardonnay is usually a safe bet except with spicy flavours when unoaked, fruity or aromatic whites work better.

Charcuterie (saucisson, salami, pâtés and air-dried hams): dry rosé and light reds like Beaujolais.

Meat-based salads with duck or chicken livers: Pinot Noir.

Cheese-based starters: with salads and cold quiches, try unoaked Chardonnay, while goats' cheese works well with Sauvignon Blanc. Champagne or sparkling wine pairs well with deep-fried cheese starters.

Vegetable-based starters: follow recommendations for cold fish-based starters. Asparagus goes well with Sauvignon Blanc.

Tapas: chilled fino or manzanilla sherry (see page 118).

Pasta, pizza and noodles

It's not the type of pasta that determines your choice of wine, it's the sauce you put with it.

Creamy sauces e.g. spaghetti carbonara: smooth, dry, Italian unoaked whites such as Soave and Pinot Bianco.

Seafood-based sauces: crisp, dry Italian whites and citrussy Sauvignon Blancs.

Tomato-based sauces: for fresh tomato sauces, crisp, dry whites such as Pinot Grigio or Sauvignon Blanc: with cooked tomato sauces, a light Italian red such as Chianti or a Barbera.

Cheese-based sauces: crisp, dry, intensely flavoured whites – good Pinot Grigio or a modern Sardinian white.

Rich meat or aubergine/eggplant-based sauces e.g. Bolognese: a fruity Italian red such as a Barbera or a Sangiovese, or a southern Italian or Sicilian red.

Baked pasta dishes e.g. meat lasagne: a good Chianti.

Pizza: generally, fruity Italian reds work better than whites.

Noodles: generally spicy, so crisp fruity whites or aromatic whites such as Riesling tend to work best.

Rice

Rice dishes work in a similar way to pasta.

Risotto: Most light vegetable and seafood risottos pair well with crisp, dry whites such as Pinot Grigio or Soave or a sparkling wine. Richer risottos based on dried mushrooms (porcini) or beet(root) can take a red (Pinot Noir and Dolcetto respectively).

Spicy rice (e.g. paella, jambalaya): dry southern French or Spanish rosé and tempranillo-based reds such as those from Rioja and Navarra.

Sushi: Muscadet or dry Champagne, especially Blanc de Blancs.

Fish

Cooked simply, fish is quite delicate, but more robust cooking techniques and saucing can call for more powerful wines.

Raw fish e.g. sushi, sashimi: see notes for Sushi, above.

Pickled fish: lager, especially pilsener, works better than wine.

Oily fish e.g. mackerel, sardines: sharp, lemony whites such as Rueda and modern Greek whites.

Smoked fish: dry Riesling or Spanish manzanilla sherry.

Salmon: served cold – unoaked Chardonnay e.g. Chablis; served hot in a pie or with pastry – lightly-oaked Chardonnay; with a hot butter sauce – a richer Chardonnay; seared or marinated with a spicy crust – a light red such as Pinot Noir.

Tuna: served cold in salad – Sauvignon Blanc or dry rosé; seared or barbecued, a chilled Pinot Noir.

Fish in a creamy sauce, including fish pie: lightly oaked Chardonnay, Chenin Blanc or oaked white Bordeaux.

Pan-fried or grilled fish: good white Burgundy or other top-quality Chardonnay, or a clean-flavoured white like Albariño.

Fish and chips and other fried fish: crisp, dry whites such as Sauvignon Blanc or a sparkling wine.

Seared, roasted or barbecued fish: a light red, such as Pinot Noir, especially if wrapped in pancetta or served with lentils.

Birds and game

Chicken

Focus on the way the chicken is cooked and the sauce that accompanies it rather than the chicken itself. See also Spicy Foods (overleaf) and recommendations for pasta (opposite).

Roast chicken: White or red Burgundy or New World Chardonnay or Pinot Noir; softer, riper styles of Bordeaux e.g. Pomerol and Merlot.

Grilled or chargrilled chicken: Will depend on the marinade – citrussy flavours suggest a crisp, fruity white like Sauvignon Blanc; a spicy marinade would work with a jammy red like Shiraz.

With tomatoes, peppers and olives: a fruity, Italian red or other Sangiovese.

Coq au vin and other red wine sauces: a similar red wine to the one you use to make the dish (perhaps a robust Rhône or Languedoc red or a Syrah).

Fried chicken: unoaked or lightly oaked Chardonnay.

Sweet and sour or fruity sauces: Fruity Australian whites such as Semillon, Semillon-Chardonnay or Colombard, or ripe, fruity reds such as Merlot.

Chicken salads: depends on the dressing. An unoaked Chardonnay or a fruity rosé will cover most eventualities but if there's a South-East Asian twist to the recipe, a Sauvignon Blanc, Riesling, Verdelho or Viognier is likely to work much better.

Turkey

See chicken, but bear in mind that on festive occasions a roast turkey is likely to be accompanied by a flavoursome stuffing, fruity cranberry sauce and richly flavoured vegetables, which call for a full-bodied red: try something like a fruity Pinot Noir, Shiraz or even Châteauneuf-du-Pape.

Duck

Pinot Noir almost always works except with duck confit, which is better with darker, more full-bodied southern French or Spanish red.

Meat

Pork

Very similar in flavour to chicken, but the extra fattiness calls for wines with a little more acidity.

Roast pork: If flavoured Italian-style with garlic and fennel, choose a dry Italian white. Otherwise try a soft, fruity red such as a Pinot Noir, Merlot or a good cru Beaujolais. Chenin Blanc and Riesling are good with cold roast pork.

Pork with apples and cider: cider is better than wine.

Sausages: robust, fruity southern French or Spanish red.

Hot gammon: a fruity red such as Merlot or a Carmenère.

Cold ham: Chablis or other unoaked Chardonnay and Beaujolais. See also Charcuterie under Starters/Appetizers.

Lamb

Roast or grilled lamb: red Bordeaux and other Cabernet- and Merlot-based wines, Rioja and Chianti Classico.

Lamb shanks and casseroles: robust, rustic reds such as those from the Rhône, Southern France and Spain.

Greek-style lamb kebabs: a fruity red or citrussy white.

Lamb tagines: Rioja Reserva or soft, pruney southern Italian reds. See also Spicy Foods.

Beef and venison

Roasts and steaks: any fine red you enjoy. Argentinian Malbec is a particularly good steak wine.

Casseroles, stews and pies: can cover quite a wide range of flavours from a beef stew with dumplings (for which beer is a better accompaniment than wine) to a rich oxtail stew (try Zinfandel). A useful guide is that if you use wine to make the stew, drink a robust red; if you use beer, drink ale.

Teriyaki or stir-fried beef: a ripe fruity red such as a Chilean or Australian Cabernet Sauvignon or a full-bodied New World Pinot Noir. See also Spicy Foods.

Veal

Similar to pork, although given the cost of veal, you might feel justified in indulging in a rather better bottle of wine!

Veal escalopes: dry Italian whites such as Pinot Grigio or an Italian red like Chianti.

Osso bucco: Italian dry whites such as Soave.

Vegetables

Vegetables are like any other ingredient – you need to think about the way they're cooked when debating what to drink.

Spring vegetables and salads e.g. asparagus, peas and broad/fava beans: crisp fresh, fruity whites such as Sauvignon Blanc and Grüner Veltliner.

Mediterranean vegetables such as tomatoes, peppers, aubergines/eggplant and courgettes/zucchini: dry rosés and medium-bodied southern French and Italian reds.

Autumn vegetables e.g. sweetcorn, squash, pumpkin and mushrooms: a buttery Chardonnay goes particularly well with the first three. A lighter Chardonnay or Pinot Noir are both good choices with mushrooms.

Winter vegetables e.g. onions, carrots, parsnips and dark leafy greens: often served in hearty dishes such as stews and soups, which tend to suit rustic reds and ales.

Vegetarian dishes: vegetarian bakes containing beans or cheese suit hearty reds, but check that they are suitable for vegetarians (i.e. no animal-derived products have been used in making them).

Cheese

Red wine isn't always the best choice with cheese, as explained on page 41.

Goats' cheese: Sauvignon Blanc and English dry whites.

Camembert and Brie-style cheeses: fruity reds such as Pinot Noir and Merlot. Cider is particularly good with Camembert.

Cheddar and other hard cheeses: aged Spanish reds such as Rioja.

Strong washed-rind cheeses such as Epoisses and Munster: strong Belgian beers work better than wine.

Blue Cheeses: sweet wines, port or sweeter sherries.

Hot cheese dishes: white wines generally work better than reds, unless it's a baked pasta dish like lasagne. For a fondue, try a really crisp, dry white like a Chasselas from Switzerland. With macaroni cheese, try a light Chardonnay.

Desserts

There are some luscious pairings to experience.

Apple, pear, peach and apricot-based desserts: simple French-style fruit tarts are the perfect foil for a great dessert wine like Sauternes. Apricot tarts work well with sweet Muscat.

Strawberry and raspberry desserts: need light, lemony dessert wines with good acidity like late-harvest Sauvignon and Riesling.

Lemon-flavoured desserts: can be tricky. Very sweet German and Austrian dessert wines work best.

Light, creamy desserts e.g. gâteaux and pavlovas: demi-sec Champagne or Moscato d'Asti.

Toffee- or caramel-flavoured desserts e.g. tarte tatin, pecan pie: late-harvested and liqueur Muscats work well with these.

Chocolate desserts: sweet reds are often easier to match than sweet whites, or a late-bottled vintage port – see page 103.

Spicy foods

Spice is not the enemy of wine that it's reputed to be as. It's only really hot chillies that cause a problem.

Mildly spiced dishes, including Middle-Eastern mezze, grills and mild Indian curries: simple, crisp fruity whites and dry rosés work best. See also Lamb Tagines.

Moderately hot curries such as Rogan Josh: inexpensive fruity New World reds such as Cabernet-Shiraz blends. With chicken curries try a Semillon-Chardonnay.

Hot curries: Tricky. Try Gewürztraminer or Pinotage. Otherwise stick to lager or the Indian yogurt-based drink, lassi.

Smoked chilli, paprika or pimentón-based dishes such as Chilli con Carne, Goulash or bean dishes flavoured with chorizo: Soft, fruity reds such as Rioja, other aged Spanish reds and Zinfandel.

Thai salads and curries: better with whites. Try Alsace Riesling and Tokay Pinot Gris or Gewürztraminer with red Thai curries.

Matching Food to Wine

Sometimes the starting point for a meal is not a menu but a wine: a treasured bottle that you've been looking for an occasion to drink, a gift that you want to share with the donor or simply a serendipitous find that inspires you to create a feast. Of course, you can enjoy it with many of the recipes in this book, particularly those in the Fine Wine Dinner (see page 144), but here are some lists of ingredients and dishes that will flatter good wines:

Whites

Chardonnay: Lighter styles such as Chablis and good white Burgundy are perfect for simple grilled fish such as plaice, dover sole or salmon, or delicate shellfish like scallops or prawns/shrimp. Richer Chardonnays are fabulous with roast or sautéed chicken or veal, especially with wild mushrooms, with creamy or buttery sauces or with rich-tasting autumnal vegetables like squash and pumpkin.

Sauvignon Blanc: Unoaked Sauvignon is perfect for healthy, fresh-tasting fish dishes such as grilled seabass, spring vegetables, especially asparagus, and goats' cheese. Oaked Sauvignons, especially those that are blended with Semillon as in Bordeaux, work with similar dishes to Chardonnay.

Riesling: Dry rieslings are shown off best by delicate seafood like fresh crab, prawns/shrimp and lightly smoked fish such as trout or salmon. Slightly sweeter styles are good with duck, goose and subtly spiced dishes with Asian influences.

Pinot Grigio/Pinot Gris: Like other dry Italian whites, Pinot Grigio is a good choice for antipasti and seafood-based pasta or risotto and grilled fish. Richer Pinot Gris, which often has a note of sweetness, works better with lightly spiced chicken and pork dishes, especially if given a South-East Asian twist.

Viognier: Works with similar dishes to Chardonnay, especially chicken, but can handle a little more spice.

Gewürztraminer: This exotically scented white isn't to everyone's taste, but it comes into its own with spicy food, especially Thai and moderately spiced Indian curries. It's also good with duck.

Reds

Pinot Noir e.g. red Burgundy: Duck is almost always a great choice with young fruity Pinot Noir as is simply roasted chicken and turkey and seared tuna. Older Pinots are good with guinea fowl and game birds such as pheasant and partridge.

Syrah/shiraz: French Syrahs such as those from the Northern Rhône are again good with red meat, but can also take more robust treatment – intensely flavoured winey stews, for example, or meat that's been cooked on a barbecue. Shiraz can take even more spice.

Cabernet Sauvignon, Merlot and blends of the two e.g. red Bordeaux: You can't go wrong with roast beef or lamb, a good steak or some simply grilled lamb chops. If you're dealing with an older vintage, keep any accompanying sauce and vegetables light – the natural meat juices are the best accompaniment.

Italian reds e.g. Barolo, top Tuscan reds like Chianti: Always best enjoyed with classic Italian food, preferably from the region. Barolo is particularly good with braised beef, game, rich pasta and truffles. Chianti shines with Italian-style roast lamb and veal and with baked pasta dishes like lasagne.

Rioja and other Spanish reds: With the revolution in Spanish winemaking, Spanish reds are changing faster than you can say paella. The typical style used to be exemplified by Rioja Reservas and Gran Reservas with their soft, delicate fruit and gentle tannins (good with grilled lamb, game, sheeps' cheeses and subtly spiced stews and tagines), but the new wave of reds can handle much more robust flavours – more like a Cabernet Sauvignon or top Tuscan red, as previously.

Zinfandel, Pinotage and other rustic reds: These are ideal for your heartiest meals like big rich meaty stews and braises. Also good with a cheeseboard.

Sweet wines: Top dessert wines like Sauternes are at their best with simple fruit tarts, especially apple, pear, peach or nectarine-based ones and strawberry tarts with crème pâtissière (cream helps to show off sweet wines). You can also drink them with foie gras or other rich liver pâtés and with blue cheese (the latter also being the classic way to enjoy vintage port).

Champagne: Champagne is a surprisingly flexible partner for food, particularly eggs and seafood and also handles Asian cuisines well, especially Chinese and Japanese food. A glass of sweet (demi-sec) Champagne is also a glamorous way to finish off a meal – it goes well with gâteaux and other celebration cakes. See Food and Fizz, page 138.

Making the most of every glass

There is nothing more enjoyable than exploring the world
of wine. After all, there can be few other subjects that consider
uncorking a bottle and pouring yourself a glass to be an essential
part of your research! Whether you want to learn a little more about
wine before you dive into the menus and their wine matches, need a
reminder of the different grapes and styles, or simply require some
advice on how best to store your wines, the following pages will act
as an indispensable guide. Simply combine this basic knowledge
with the delicious menus contained in this book, and you will find
that many pleasurable hours with food, wine and friends await you.

Choosing Wine by Style

Choosing wine that you will enjoy becomes easier once you understand that most wines fall into one of several main style groups. Try to identify your own preferences as well as those of your guests and then take into account that wine is made to be drunk with food – some styles will pair better with certain foods and also suit the style of occasion more than others (see pages 6–13).

Sparkling wines

With the cheerful sound of the popping cork and the fizz tumbling into the glass, sparkling wine is the perfect choice for any celebration, and most people will be delighted to receive it as a gift. Most dry sparkling wine, including Champagne, Cava, Prosecco, and wines from England, Australia, New Zealand and South Africa, can be drunk alone or accompany light nibbles or canapés. Some richer styles – particularly vintage Champagne –

can work well with light starters and salads. When choosing Champagne, it can be worth seeking out the slightly smaller houses such as Ruinart, Pol Roger, Gosset and Billecart-Salmon, all of which produce good non-vintage wines. Prosecco and Cava are particularly nice to serve with light bites from their country of origin (Spain and Italy respectively). Sparkling wines, including Champagne, are often dry, but also come in semi-sweet (or demi-sec) and sweet styles, both of which are a great choice for serving with cake or dessert, or after dinner on their own. Pink sparkling wines can be dry or sweet, so be sure to check the label carefully.

Light whites

Light-bodied white wines are perfect as an apéritif in summer, or served with canapés, vegetable-based first courses, salads or light shellfish such as oysters. Light, dry wines to look for include whites from the Loire valley in northern France, such as Muscadet; inexpensive white Bordeaux; Chablis (which is particularly good with oysters); white wines from northern Italy, and some English white wines such as Chapel Down. It's also worth looking out for light, slightly sweet (sometimes known as 'off-dry') wines with good acidity, which can also be delicious served as an apéritif, such as German Riesling or French Vouvray.

Grassy whites

Grassy, aromatic whites, typically made from grape varieties such as Sauvignon Blanc, Pinot Gris or Grüner Veltliner, are versatile and often a good choice for people who don't like heavily oaked wines. They tend to have good acidity, a characteristic grassy, fresh and herbaceous aroma, and sufficient body to work with a variety of different types of food. Look for the classic French wines made with Sauvignon Blanc, such as Sancerre, Menetou-Salon and Pouilly Fumé, all of which are great with goats' cheese, salmon or smoked fish, or the richer, more aromatic Sauvignon Blanc and Pinot Gris from New Zealand and South Africa, which can be great with spicy or Asian-influenced food made with chicken and fish.

Full-bodied, oaky whites

Some of the best known and most delicious white wines of all are full-bodied and oaked to varying degrees, notably the classic French whites such as Meursault, Pouilly-Fuissé and other Burgundies, which are predominantly made from Chardonnay grapes. Further south, Condrieu, made from Viognier, is rich and apricot-like, but still dry. White Rioja can be a good choice, too. Rich and rounded in flavour and subtle golden yellow in colour, these wines are great with classic French cooking, creamy sauces, roast chicken, rich white fish and shellfish, and even pork. Also look out for rich, oaked Chardonnays and Viogniers from France, Australia, South Africa and Chile.

Rich or sweet whites

There is a huge range of rich or sweet white wines, all of which can be drunk in several different ways. Look out for grape varieties like Gewürztraminer and Riesling, often encountered in wines from Alsace and Germany, and the South American Torrontés, widely grown in Argentina. These are usually slightly sweet and very expressive and aromatic, but still have good acidity, which helps them work even with curries and dishes containing chilli. Other even richer and sweeter wines are made from grapes with botrytis, or noble rot, which concentrates the grape juice while the grapes are on the vine, thereby making the wine sweeter. Such wines can be delicious with rich desserts, dried fruit and some cheeses, especially blue cheese. Wines to look for include Sauternes, Monbazillac, Coteaux du Layon and many others made in the same way in Australia, New Zealand and South Africa. They will have a rich, deep golden colour and a delicious honeyed or raisin-like aroma. Try vins doux naturels, too. .These are lightly fortified wines, often made from Muscat grapes, which are slightly less sweet than the noble rot wines, and are delicious with lighter desserts such as fresh berries, jellies and pannacotta.

Light and fruity reds

Light and fruity reds are the perfect summer drink, and many of them are best served chilled. They work well on their own as an apéritif, or with platters of light meats and charcuterie, grilled vegetables or other antipasti. Classic examples to look for include the celebrated Beaujolais and wines from other countries

made with the Gamay grape. Some Pinot Noirs, especially those from New Zealand and North America, and young Italian reds made from the Sangiovese grape, are wonderfully light and fruity. Look out, too, for the light red wines from the Loire valley in France, including Chinon and red Sancerre.

Soft, mellow or medium-bodied reds

Soft, mellow, medium-bodied reds can provide very easy drinking and are great paired with food of a similar weight – in other words, pasta, especially with tomato and meat-based sauces, rare roast beef, and light grilled or barbecued meats. They can also work well with richer vegetable-based dishes such as aubergine/eggplant parmigiana. Good wines to choose would be the lighter red Bordeaux, Spanish wines made with Tempranillo, including the most famous of all, Rioja; many country reds, or vins de pays, from southern France; Merlots from Chile and North America; and Chianti and other mid-weight Italian reds.

Juicy, fruit-forward, full-bodied reds

Many red wines from Australia, New Zealand, South Africa and South and North America, especially California, are juicy, fruit-driven and full-bodied, and have won a lot of fans for their easy-going accessibility. The grape varieties to look out for are Merlot, Cabernet Sauvignon, Grenache and Cabernet Franc. Some Italian reds, such as Rosso de Montalcino, also fall into this category. These wines are good paired with food of a similar weight, such as game, roast lamb, lentils, sausages and other rustic, full-flavoured dishes.

Big, powerful or spicy reds

If you enjoy big, spicy reds, Shiraz (or Syrah in France) is the grape variety to look for. It is spicy in all its incarnations, and more often than not it's full-bodied and robust too. It's good paired with slow-roast red meats, robust stews and casseroles, and rare red meat. French Syrah from the Rhône Valley is well worth exploring, such as Côte-Rôtie and Hermitage; so too is Shiraz from Australia, California and South Africa. The Grenache grape (known as Garnacha in Spain) is also a good choice, and makes up a good proportion of the blend of grapes in the classic French Châteauneuf-du-Pape. Other powerful reds to look out for include Malbec from Argentina – a classic pairing with steak – South African Pinotage, Spanish Priorat, and wines made from the Nebbiolo grape in Italy, such as Barolo.

Rosé

Rosé wines have grown enormously in popularity in recent years, and are made in countless different styles. They range from bone dry to very sweet, vary in colour from a faint salmon-pink blush to a pale red, and are made with several different grape varieties. Rosé can be a very versatile choice and will successfully accompany a wide range of foods, depending on how dry or sweet it is, and how full-bodied. It's wise to check the label for as much information as you can before choosing. Light, pale, dry rosés from Provence and other areas of France are often made with Pinot Noir, and are great with light pasta dishes, seafood or salads. Light, semi-sweet or 'off-dry' styles, including Rosé d'Anjou and many Portugese rosés, can work well with lightly spiced dishes and light curries, and can also be very good with light desserts such as fresh berries. Dry, medium-bodied

rosés, including those from the southern Rhône and Spain, can be great with pork and seafood, as can Zinfandel rosé from North America, although some of the big-name brands can be a little sweet. Full-bodied, fruity rosés, including the more expensive Provençal appellations such as Bandol, and those made in Australia from Shiraz and Cabernet Sauvignon, are often good with barbecued fish and meats, or light curries.

Fortified wines

Fortified wines are those to which a distilled alcohol, such as brandy, has been added. There are lots of different styles to choose from, but some of the best known are port, sherry, Madeira, Marsala and vermouth. Fortified wine makes an excellent gift, and comes in as many styles as there are occasions to serve it at. The main styles of sherry to look out for are dry Fino and Amontillado, the slightly darker and richer Oloroso and Palo Cortado, and the sweet Pedro Ximénez and cream sherries. The main styles of port are tawny port, which is aged in barrels and can be sweet or medium-dry; ruby port, which is bottle-aged and is usually sweet; late bottled vintage (LBV) port, which has been aged from 4–6 years; vintage port, the product of a single vintage and the most renowned style; and finally white port, which can be dry or sweet and is made from white grapes. When it comes to drinking fortified wines, a light, well-chilled vermouth such as Noilly Prat or Martini, or a dry sherry is a good choice for a refreshing apéritif. Port or Madeira, or a richer style of sherry, are wonderful served after dinner and can make any occasion feel special. Some ports and sherries are perfect partners with cheese, too, and are worth considering if you are planning a cheese board.

Reading Bottles and Labels

Aside from their obvious visual appeal, some wine labels can be confusing, or may even look daunting. It's worth paying attention to them, though, as even the plainest will reveal something about its contents. The bottle itself can be an indicator, too, both in terms of the shape and the type of glass it is made from.

Bottles

Once you start to look at them more closely, you'll notice that wine bottles vary in shape a lot more than you might have thought. This is partly for practical reasons: some bottles will have a thick layer of glass on the base for reinforcement, and the base will be concave to varying degrees to offer a better grip when opening it, particularly in the case of Champagne bottles. The colour of the glass will also change according to the contents: white wines are usually in pale green or sometimes transparent glass; rosés are nearly always in transparent glass to show off the colour; while reds are usually in dark green or brown glass. There are also a few different bottle shapes that are traditionally associated with different types of wine. The classic straight-sided bottle with distinctive shoulders near the top is used in Bordeaux, while bottles with more gently sloping sides are used in Burgundy. Tall, slender bottles are traditionally used in Germany, and have become associated with sweet wine as a result, but they are not always an indicator of sweetness. Wine-producing countries outside France and Germany have fewer bottle-shape allegiances, so the choice of shape is often an indication of the style of wine inside.

Labels

Labels vary hugely, but even the sparest will tell you the name of the wine, where it was made, the alcoholic strength and the quantity of it in the bottle. In addition, many labels will include a date or vintage, a quality classification, a grape variety or region, an indication of the sweetness level and a tasting note on the back label. The main difference you'll notice between French and non-French wines is that French wines are named after the region (or appellation), and don't usually mention a grape variety, whereas wines from other parts of the world often do. This reflects the French emphasis on terroir, or the individual characteristics of the area in which the wine was produced, rather than grape variety, but it can make French wines a little more difficult to choose. One way round this is to remember the name of a French wine you particularly like, and then look out for wines made in the less well-known neighbouring regions, which are often similar in style and can be less expensive.

Quality classifications

The issue of quality classifications can be confusing. The systems in each country are not directly comparable, but the basic principles are the same — the intention is to offer a guarantee of a certain quality level by giving accreditations only to wines produced in a limited geographical area, and/or following certain rules (which may include the percentage of different grape varieties that can be used, the harvesting method, or any additives that may or may not be used). There are some key quality classifications that are helpful to look out for. The most sophisticated and complicated classifications are European, but some of the more recent wine-producing countries have also started to develop their own, which are usually less restrictive, such as the AVA (American Viticultural Area) in North America.

In France, the top-level classification is AOC, or Appellation d'Origine Contrôllée, which is followed by VDQS, or Vin Délimité de Qualité Superieure, Vin de Pays and Vin de Table, in descending order. From 2012 the wine classifications are to be revised, and AOP (Appellation d'Origine Protégée) will gradually replace AOC, IGP (Indication Géographique) will replace Vin de Pays, and Vin de Table will become Vin de France.

The classifications in Germany are less related to regions, and more to do with production methods, quality guarantees and sweetness levels. The top-level classification is Prädikatswein (formerly Qualitätswein mit Prädikat, or QmP), followed by Qualitätswein bestimmter Anbaugebiete, or QbA. The next two classifications are Deutscher Landwein and Deutscher Tafelwein, which roughly correspond with the bottom two French classifications. You'll also see indications relating to sweetness levels, ranging from dry (Trocken), to dry or off-dry (Kabinett), to Spätlese, Auslese and Beerenauslese, all of which refer to increasing levels of sweetness.

In Spain Denominación de Origin (DO) signifies quality wine produced in a specified region. Spain boasts over 50 DO zones, each with its own regulatory body which agrees on permitted grape varieties and maximum yields. Denominación de Origin Calificada (DOCa) is a higher category which was awarded first to Rioja and more recently to the Priorat region. This is awarded when a region has demonstrated high quality over a number of years. Vino de la Tierra (VdlT), meaning 'wine of the land', can be compared to the French Vin de Pays. At least 60% of the wine must come from a specified region which isn't yet DO status but does have a local character. There are over 20 VdlT areas. Vino de Mesa (VdM) is a basic table wine and can be blended from more than one region or grape variety. The vintage is not stated on the label. Quality Spanish reds are also classified by age, which is stated on the label. Wines labelled Crianza spend two years maturing, with a minimum of six months in an oak cask and the remainder in bottle or vat. A Reserva spends three years

developing, at least one of which must be in a cask and at least one in a bottle. Gran Reserva are only made in the best vintages and from the best grapes. Ageing takes place for at least two years in oak and a further three in the bottle, though most Gran Reserva wines will be much older.

In Italy, the top level is DOCG (Denominazione di Origine Controllata e Garantita), followed by DOC (Denominazione di Origine Controllata), then IGT (Indicazione Geografica Tipica) and VDT (Vino da Tavola). There is also a group of wines known as the 'Super Tuscans', the most famous being Tignanello and Sassicaia, which are made in Tuscany by producers who choose not to follow the rules laid down by the region. Despite being of very high quality, they were originally labelled as VDT, and the IGT designation was partly created so they could be included within the classification system.

Other quality designations to look out for on sparkling wine labels include méthode champenoise or méthode traditionelle, both of which indicates that the wine has been made in the same way as Champagne – in other words, using bottle fermentation to create the bubbles, rather than being artificially carbonated. The designation 'NV' on Champagne labels means non-vintage – in other words the wine is made from a blend of different vintages, or years. Extra-brut, brut nature and non dosé all mean extra-dry; brut means dry; sec means dryish, demi-sec means medium sweet, and doux means sweet.

Where to Buy

Good-quality wine is now more accessible than ever, and for a range of budgets and confidence levels, thanks to the huge variety on offer at independent wine merchants, high-street off-licence/liquor stores and supermarkets, as well as online mail order firms and wine clubs. Wine auctions, too, can be a lot of fun for the more knowledgeable wine enthusiast.

Independent wine merchants

Independent wine merchants can be a great place to start if you'd like to explore wines a little more – the staff are likely to be extremely knowledgeable and passionate about their subject, and will probably be more than happy to spend time giving helpful advice and suggestions. Some even organize regular wine tastings and events for their customers. You're likely to find a whole range of interesting wines from small producers here, too, although they may be a little more expensive than the supermarket. Don't be afraid to ask for advice or suggestions about what to serve, or for new things to try if you want to explore a particular grape variety or region. Since the stock may be on the shelves for slightly longer in independent wine shops/stores, look out for signs of badly kept bottles, such as any seepage from the cork, or dried out or damaged closures.

High-street retailers

Off-licences/liquor stores can vary enormously in the quality and range of wines they stock. You may find that they have a smaller selection than the large supermarkets, but they will usually be able to offer things that you won't find there, and will stock a whole range of wines, fortified wines and spirits, from the big-name producers to smaller vineyards. They should also be able to offer some advice or make recommendations if you're in need of inspiration, and it's always worth looking out for special offers, as these may highlight the particular favourites of the staff. Bear in mind that the more we support our local wine suppliers, the more likely we are to end up with a decent selection of interesting wines in our neighbourhood.

Supermarkets

The range of wines available in supermarkets has greatly improved in recent years, as their customers have requested better quality and more choice. Supermarkets do tend to focus on the lower price points and well-known brands rather than small producers, but they can be a great source of classic wines, and will reliably stock the big-name brands. Supermarket own-label wines can also offer very good quality and represent excellent value, and are often made by the same big producers that make wines whose names you might recognize. Look out for the special offers, which will generally represent genuinely good value for everyday wines; at the same time, though, you're unlikely to unearth any hidden gems. Some larger supermarkets will have wine advisers on hand to answer your questions and make recommendations.

Mail order/internet

Mail-order companies can be an extremely practical, if slightly less personal, way of buying wine – and of course, having it delivered straight to your door can be very helpful. There's usually a minimum order of half a case (six bottles), but many companies have regular special offers and sell fairly inexpensive mixed cases of everyday red, rosé and white, which can be great value and a good way to experiment with new wines that you might not find in the supermarket. And, of course, wine enthusiasts can usually track down the exact hard-to-find bottle that they've been searching for online. Several of the larger independent wine merchants have excellent online stores. There is usually more information about each wine on a website than you'd find in a shop, which will help you decide what to buy, although of course the downside is that it is difficult to ask for advice. It's therefore advisable stick to the better known, larger mail order firms to begin with.

Buying at auction

Wines are often sold at auction, both by the barrel or by the bottle (usually by the case), at established auction houses or sometimes directly by the winery. Auctioned wines are usually fine, collectible or specialist wines, which are often intended for ageing and may increase in value considerably – in fact, some buyers are there purely for the investment potential, rather than to fill their cellars. However, wine auctions aren't only for the experts, and they can be a great way to learn more about wine, as well as experiencing the wine world at first hand. If you are a novice, do your homework by going along to an auction to see how it operates before you decide to bid. You will either find the catalogue online or printed catalogues will be available. Some auctions feature small sales, which often include good-value mixed lots. It's best to choose a well-known auction house and to check that the wine has been stored and handled well; the bottles should have been stored on their sides, and there should be no signs of seepage, damaged closures, or excessive ullage (the amount of space at the top of the bottle), except in the case of very old bottles. When buying wine at auction, bear in mind that the price you bid is not generally the price you pay – you will also be liable for a buyer's premium and tax.

Glasses

It's surprising how much difference serving your wines in fine-quality glasses can make, but the good news is that they don't have to cost a fortune. The right glasses will show off the wine's appearance, and their rounded shape will trap and release the aroma to the nose. Don't be tempted to fill them up too much – remember to leave plenty of room for the wine to express itself!

Wine can be served in glasses of all shapes and sizes, from enormous round goblets to small chunky tumblers. It's largely a matter of personal preference and budget, and also depends on how much room you have to store your glassware.

Many wine aficionados prefer to drink from large glasses made with very thin glass, so that as little as possible comes between them and their beloved liquid! If you are interested in wine, it is

certainly worth giving some consideration to the most appropriate type of glasses to buy. The basic small, round wine glass with a short stem is called the Paris goblet, which is practical and serviceable but does not give you much space to swirl the wine around inside the glass. The standard glass shape used for wine industry tastings is the ISO tasting glass, which is also quite small, but has a thinner, taller, tulip-shaped bowl to contain the wine while it is swirled, and to funnel the aromas up towards the nose.

The ideal wine glass shape is considered to be wider towards the bottom (the bowl) with a narrower opening at the top. In general, white wine glasses are often slightly taller, narrower and more upright in shape, while red wine glasses tend to be larger, fuller and rounder with a wider bowl to help accumulate the aromas, and a larger opening to allow you to dip your nose into the glass. A classic Bordeaux glass is tall with a large bowl, while a Burgundy glass has a broader bowl to help contain the delicate flavour compounds. Rustic or table wines, especially reds, are also sometimes served in tumblers, especially in rustic

Italian or Spanish restaurants, although the shape of a tumbler will not do a great deal to help the wine.

Champagne and sparkling wine are always best served in tall, slender glasses known as flutes rather than the wide, shallow-bowled, old-fashioned champagne coupe (which, legend has it, was modelled on the breast of Marie Antoinette). This is because flutes show off the tall lines of bubbles (known as the 'mousse') better, and also preserve the wine's fizz by having a smaller surface area on which the bubbles can pop.

One of the best-known manufacturers of wine glasses is Riedel, who make glasses in all shapes and sizes. Whatever size, shape or style of glass you choose, remember that when drinking wine you should hold it by the stem, rather than by the bowl, so that the heat of your hands does not affect the temperature of the wine, and so that you can see the colour of the wine clearly. The best way to clean wine glasses and keep them sparkling is to wash them in hot soapy water, give them a quick rinse in cold water and then dry them immediately with a clean tea towel.

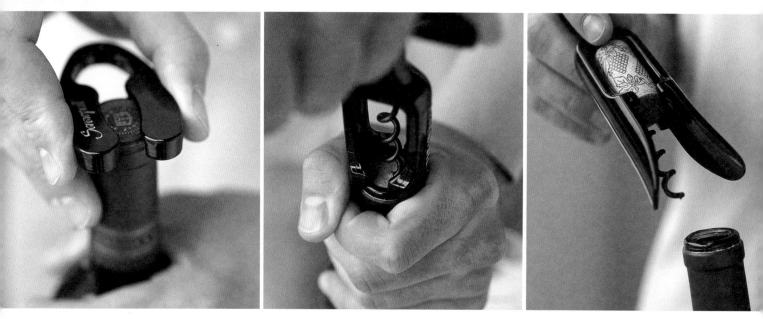

Equipment

Serving wine does not require any fancy equipment – a few glasses and a corkscrew are all you really need (and often not even a corkscrew, thanks to screw cap bottles). However, it's worth knowing about some of the other equipment available, which can make serving wine even easier and more pleasurable.

The first challenge when opening wine is to find a good corkscrew. There are many different types, with varying degrees of engineering complexity, but the main thing here is to identify a style that you find simple and easy to use. For many people, that's just the basic bartenders' corkscrew with its attached lever to help you prise the cork out of the bottle. Foil cutters, which fit round the neck of the bottle and make a clean cut through the foil a few millimetres below the top of the neck, can also be useful and are often used by professionals to make sure the foil stays looking nice while ensuring that it never comes into contact with the wine. When it comes to pouring, flexible stainless steel funnels inserted into the neck of the bottle can be useful to ensure an even pour and to help you prevent any drips or splashes.

Wine coolers or wine buckets are useful to help keep wine at the right temperature on, or next to, the table, although some people prefer to be able to see the wine bottle easily. If you use a wine bucket, it's best to have a clean cloth handy to soak up any drips.

Decanters are the classic piece of wine equipment, and they can add enormously to the pleasure of drinking fine wine. Any attractive glass jug can be used, although specialist decanters are often designed to show off the wine to its best advantage, and to provide a wide surface area for maximum aeration. Stoppered decanters are useful for fortified wines or those you may not drink in one sitting. When checking for sediment, a strong table lamp, or even a large candle, can be useful for revealing any sediment in the wine and thus avoid pouring it into the decanter (see page 33). A coffee filter paper can be handy, too – if the cork has crumbled into the bottle, just pour the wine through the paper into the decanter or jug. Decanters are notoriously tricky to clean; some people recommend standing them in denture-cleaning solution, and tiny metal cleaning balls are also available, which you swirl around inside the decanter and then pour out into a sieve.

Opening, Decanting and Serving

Part of the pleasure of serving any wine is the ritual of opening it – the pop of the cork and the glug of the wine as it's poured into the glass. But corks can be problematic and unreliable as closures, and it's for this reason that many wines (and not just inexpensive ones) are now sealed with metal screw caps.

Opening sparkling wine

All sparkling wine should be opened with great care. Have the glasses waiting nearby so that you can start pouring the wine immediately after opening it. The best way to open a bottle of sparkling wine is to untwist the foil, remove the wire seal and keep your thumb over the cork. Hold the bottle firmly by the base and make sure it is pointed away from you and any other people. Gently twist the base of the bottle to release the cork, and hold it down as you feel it coming out so that it is released from the bottle with a gentle hiss, not an explosive pop. Half-fill the glasses, pouring in the wine at an angle to avoid creating too much mousse, then go back and top them up again afterwards.

Ice buckets and coolers

If you don't have time to pre-chill wine in the fridge, the most effective way to cool it down quickly is to use a wine bucket filled up with ice and water. This should cool most wines within about 15 minutes. Another trick is to wrap the bottle in a wet tea towel and place it in the freezer for a few minutes.

Decanting

There are many and various reasons for decanting wine; one of the main ones is simply to enjoy the vivid, sparkling colour. Some younger, powerful red wines will also benefit from a small amount of aeration, which is provided by pouring the wine into the decanter and letting it sit untouched for a short while. If you are decanting for this reason, splash the wine against the side of the decanter as you pour it in. Decanting can also help remove any sediment from the wine. This is usually done by first ensuring that the wine has been stored upright for a few days, then pouring it slowly into the decanter in front of a light source placed by the neck of the bottle to help you identify where the sediment is and stop pouring before it comes out. Most wines, especially old and fragile ones, should be decanted very shortly before serving. Some younger, tough red wines will benefit from being decanted 3–4 hours before drinking as the exposure to oxygen will soften the tannins.

Serving temperature

The easiest thing you can do to enhance any wine and make sure you enjoy it at its best is to serve it at the right temperature. The basic principles are that the cooler the wine is, the less acidic or sweet it is perceived to be, and less aroma will be released. Crisp, dry whites and sparkling wines are usually served coolest and flavoursome, aged reds the warmest. Warmer temperatures also help tannins relax, thereby bringing out the best in powerful reds. Most sweet wines are best served chilled, as are rosés and many light reds.

Suggested chilling times for whites and rosés

Light, sweet white wines: around 2 hours in the fridge

Sparkling and dessert wines: around 2 hours in the fridge

Light, dry whites: around 1½ hours in the fridge

Medium-bodied whites and rosés: around 1 hour in the fridge

Full-bodied, rich whites and rosés: around 45 minutes in the fridge

Suggested chilling times for red wine

Light reds: around 45 minutes in the fridge

Medium-bodied reds: around 15–30 minutes in the fridge

Full-bodied reds: cool room temperature

Glossary of Wine Terms

Acidity A feature of most wines, natural acids give wine character and structure, and help it age.

Aerate Bring a wine into contact with air to accelerate its development.

Alcohol The sugar in ripe grapes turns into alcohol to produce wine.

Aroma The smell of a wine.

Bianco (Italian) White.

Blanc (French) White.

Blanco (Spanish) White.

Blend Mixture of more than one grape variety.

Blind tasting Wine tasting at which labels and shapes of bottles are concealed from tasters.

Body Weight and structure of a wine.

Botrytis cinerea Fungus that shrivels and rots white grapes, concentrating their flavours and sugars. It creates dessert wines high in alcohol and richness of flavour. Also known as noble rot, pourriture noble and edelfäule.

Bouquet Complex scent of a wine that develops as it matures.

Château (French) Wine-growing property, usually in Bordeaux.

Claret Red wine from Bordeaux.

Complex (said of a wine) Marked by a variety of flavours.

Concentrated (said of a wine) Marked by depth, richness and fruitiness.

Core Colour of wine in the centre of a glass.

Corkage Charge per bottle levied on customers in restaurants who bring in their own wine to drink.

Corked Condition, revealed by a musty odour, where a wine has been contaminated by a faulty cork.

Côte (French) Hillside of vineyards.

Crémant (French) Semi-sparkling.

Cru (French) Growth or vineyard.

Cuvée (French) Blended wine or special selection.

Demi-sec (French) Semi-sweet.

Dolce (Italian) Sweet.

Domaine (French) Property or estate.

Doux (French) Sweet.

Dulce (Spanish) Sweet.

Fermentation Transformation of grape juice into wine, whereby yeasts, which are naturally present in grapes and occasionally added in cultured form, convert sugars into alcohol.

Flavour Aroma and taste of a wine, which is often compared to fruits, spices and so on.

Fortified wine Wine – such as port, sherry, or madeira – to which alcohol has been added either to stop it from fermenting before all its sugars turn to alcohol or simply to strengthen it.

Frizzante (Italian) Semi-sparkling.

Full-bodied (said of wine) Marked by a high level of fruit concentration and alcohol.

Grand cru (French) Top-quality wines from Alsace, Bordeaux, Burgundy and Champagne.

Halbtrocken (German) Medium dry.

Landwein (German) A level of quality wine just above simple table wine, equivalent to the French vin de pays.

Late harvest (said of grapes) Very ripe grapes that have been picked late when their sweetness is most concentrated.

Méthode champenoise Method by which Champagnes and top-quality sparkling wines are made; involves a secondary fermentation in bottle.

Moelleux (French) Sweet.

Mousse (French) The fizz in a glass of sparkling wine as it is poured.

Mousseux (French) Sparkling.

Noble rot Botrytis cinera fungus, which attacks grape skins and results in super-concentration.

Non-vintage (NV) A wine that is a blend of more than one vintage, notably champagne.

Nose The qualities of a wine that create the sensation experienced by smelling it. This is not just a matter of the wine's scent; the nose also conveys information about its condition.

Oak Wine aged in oak barrels can be identified by whiffs of vanilla or cedarwood.

Oxidized (said of wine) Wine that has deteriorated as a result of its overexposure to air.

Palate Taste of a wine in the mouth.

Pétillant (French) Slightly sparkling.

Rich (said of wine) With a good concentration of ripe fruit.

Rosso (Italian) Red.

Rouge (French) Red.

Sec (French) Dry.

Secco (Italian) Dry.

Seco (Spanish/Portuguese) Dry.

Sediment Deposit that forms after a wine has spent a long time in a bottle.

Sekt (German) Sparkling wine.

Smooth (said of wine) With good fruit levels and soft, integrated tannins.

Soft (said of wine) Rounded, fruity, low in tannin.

Sparkling (said of wine) Produced to have bubbles.

Spritzer Refreshing drink made from white wine and club soda or sparkling spring water, and often served with ice.

Spumante (Italian) Sparkling.

Sulphur Pungent smell given off by wine that can be dispersed by swirling the glass.

Sur lie (said of wine) Aged on its lees, or sediment, before bottling, resulting in a greater depth of flavour.

Tannin Austere acid found in some red wines that derives from grape skins and stalks combined with the oak barrels in which the wine has been aged; it is a necessary preservative.

Tafelwein (German) Table wine.

Terroir (French) Meaning literally 'soil' or 'earth,' terroir encompasses climate, drainage, position and anything else that distinguishes the taste of a wine from that of its immediate neighbours which have been grown and produced in the same way.

Texture What a wine feels like in the mouth; it is often compared to the feel of fabrics.

Tinto (Spanish/Portuguese) Red.

Trocken (German) Dry.

Ullage Amount of air in a bottle or barrel between the top of the wine and the base of the cork or bung.

Varietal Wine named after the grape (or the major constituent grape) from which it is made.

Variety Breed of grape.

Vendange (French) Harvest or vintage.

Vendange tardive (French) Late harvest.

Vin de pays (French) Country wine of a level higher than table wine.

Vin de table (French) Table wine.

Vin doux naturel (VDN) (French) Fortified wine that has been sweetened and strengthened by the addition of alcohol, either before or after fermentation.

Vinification Winemaking.

Vino da tavola (Italian) Table wine.

Vino de mesa (Spanish) Table wine.

Vintage Year of a grape harvest and the wine made from the grapes of that harvest.

Viscosity Thickness in a wine with a great density of fruit extract and alcohol – indicated by 'tears' or 'legs' on the side of the glass.

Viticulture Cultivation of grapes.

Weight Body and/or strength of a wine.

Winery Winemaking establishment.

Frequently Asked Questions

What sort of wine glasses do I need?

Ideally, it's useful to have four different types – a generously sized wine glass for red wines, a smaller one for white wines, a set of tall Champagne flutes and a set of smaller glasses for sherry, port and dessert wines. (See pages 28–29 for more detailed information.)

How long do I need to chill wine for?

It depends entirely on the wine. Most people tend to serve white wines too cold and red wines too warm. Champagne and dessert wines need chilling longest (about 1½–2 hours, depending on the temperature of your fridge), crisp dry whites need about about 1–1½ hours, full-bodied whites and light reds require about 45 minutes to an hour. Even full-bodied reds will benefit from being served cool rather than at room temperature (about 15–18°C), so keep them in a cooler area before serving.

How much wine should I pour in a glass?

Don't fill it more than two-thirds full. Not out of meanness, but so that you can appreciate its aromas.

How long before the meal should I open red wine?

Its only worth opening them ahead if you're planning to decant them. Otherwise not much air can get into the bottle. Most wines are designed to be drunk direct from the bottle these days.

When should I decant a wine?

Only when it's very full bodied and tannic or has thrown a deposit like vintage port. Be careful about decanting older reds. If they're very old and fragile, they may lose their delicate flavours when exposed to air.

How do I do it?

Leave the bottle upright for at least 24 hours before you plan to serve it, so that any deposit can settle. Then, with a light behind the neck of the bottle, pour the wine slowly and steadily into the decanter without stopping until you see the sediment start to inch towards the neck of the bottle.

How do I tell if a wine is corked?

If it tastes musty or stale, there almost certainly is something wrong with it and you're perfectly within your rights to reject it (so long as you don't drink half the bottle first!). If it's simply too sweet or too sharp for your taste, then you've got no real grounds to send it back. The grey area is with older wines or ones made from less common grape varieties that may have funky flavours that aren't to your taste. But if a supplier or restaurant values your goodwill, they will replace it.

If I'm invited to dinner should I take a bottle and, if so, what type?

It depends on how well you know your hosts. If you don't know them well, you don't want to imply that they won't serve you a decent bottle, so it's better to take something indulgent like a bottle of Champagne or a special dessert wine that could be construed as a gift. With good friends it's fine to ask what they'd like you to bring or what they're making so that you can choose something appropriate.

How many bottles should I take?

It depends on the numbers. For four of you one bottle is fine, although if you're cautious by nature you could always take a back-up in case one is corked. For six or eight people you might want to take two (it's better to take two bottles of the same type so that everyone gets a chance to try it).

Should I open the wine my guests have brought with them?

This is the trickiest issue, I find! I think it depends entirely on how it's presented. If they bring along an unchilled and wrapped bottle of Champagne, I think it's fair to accept that it is intended as a private treat to enjoy on another occasion. If guests produce a bottle that they're clearly excited about, the indications are that they will want to share it with you.

Pairing Cheese with Wine

Cheese and wine are classic partners, but where to begin with the seemingly endless choices for both? It's not always the perfect marriage it's held up to be and putting together a cheeseboard can be tricky, especially if it includes many different varieties of cheese. But there are many good matches to be made whether you are drinking red, white, sweet, rosé, sparkling or fortified wines, so look to the guides in the following pages to help pair your favourite wines with a huge variety of the world's cheeses. Also included are ideas for seasonal cheeseboards to serve at the end of meals and a section on entertaining solely with perfect cheese and wine pairings.

Red Wine and Cheese

People want to drink red wine with cheese, full stop. It's such a long-held belief that the two go well together that it cannot easily be dislodged. But to avoid the almost inevitable disappointment that ensues, choose your cheeses and their accompaniments carefully.

There are three useful tips to bear in mind when choosing cheese to serve with a red wine.

1. It's better to go for a hard rather than a soft or semi-soft cheese.
2. Remember that it is easier to match red wine with cooked cheese dishes than with uncooked cheese, especially when the dish features red wine-friendly ingredients, such as beef or mushrooms.
3. It helps to introduce other elements on the plate that will assist the match. Breads of character, such as walnut or sourdough (especially grilled), good farmhouse butter and cooked fruits, such as pears in red wine and cherry compote, will all help kick your wine into touch, as will a few marinated black olives, if you like them. Oh, and don't be afraid to serve a single cheese on its own – the 'hero' cheeseboard!

Cheeses that work best with red wine

- Hard sheeps' cheese, e.g. Italian Pecorino, Manchego and Zamorano from Spain, Vermont Shepherd from the US and British Berkswell: sheep's cheese is a consistently successful match with red wine
- Well-aged cheeses that have a dry, crystalline texture, e.g. Parmigiano-Reggiano, aged Gouda and Mimolette and Sbrinz from Italy, Holland, France and Switzerland respectively. Younger versions of these cheeses will also match quite well
- Mellow, medium-matured British territorial cows' cheeses, such as milder Cheddar, Cheshire and Red Leicester
- Red wine-washed cheeses such as the Italian Ubriaco and Spanish Murcia al Vino (but not white wine-, brine-, beer- or cider-washed ones)
- Mature or wrapped goats' cheeses like Banon
- Provolone piccante

Cheeses to avoid with red wine

- Very oozy Brie- and Camembert-style cheeses
- Pungent washed-rind cheeses, such as Epoisses or Langres
- Strong blues, such as Gorgonzola piccante or Roquefort

Red wines that work best with cheese

- Aged Tempranillo-based reds, such as Rioja Reserva and Gran Reserva
- Mid-weight Grenache-based reds, such as Côtes du Rhône and modern Spanish Garnacha
- Mourvèdre-based reds, such as Bandol
- Slightly 'porty' reds with rich brambly or figgy flavours, such as Douro reds, Zinfandel and Amarone, and southern Italian reds, such as Aglianico and Negroamaro
- There are circumstances in which other styles of red will work perfectly well with cheese too. Light, fruity reds, such as those from the Loire Valley and Beaujolais regions of France are good with goats' cheese, for example
- Inexpensive fruity reds, such as Chilean Pinot Noir, Merlot and Carmenère can be enjoyable with a milder Brie or Camembert
- A mature red Bordeaux can work well if none of the cheeses is too pungent. A six-year-old Canon-Fronsac can be successfully matched with a cheese board of Appleby's Cheshire, Waterloo (a buttery semi-soft cows' milk cheese), Berkswell and Cashel Blue. The key is that the cheeses are all mellow and the wine has no harsh tannins
- Even tannic young Cabernet Sauvignon, probably the most difficult red to pair with cheese, comes into its own with a steak or burger topped with melted blue cheese

If you enjoy red wine and cheese but not always the two together, just try out the recommendations and keep on experimenting until you find some pairings that work for you.

White Wine and Cheese

Once you've tried white wine with cheese, you'll never look back. The first experience is likely to be a glass of Sauvignon Blanc with a goats' cheese, an epiphany that should convert you at first sip. And once you've tried a crisp, fruity white with a fondue, or an Alsace you'll wonder why anyone drinks anything else.

The reason people are sceptical about accompanying cheese with white wine is that it seems slightly awkward to introduce a white wine at the end of a meal in which a full-bodied red has been served with the main course; you don't want to switch back to a light, crisp white. But there are many lighter meals with which you might be drinking white and carry on doing so through the cheese course, or simple snacks where all you need to do is pull a bottle of white wine from the fridge. It's well worth planning a meal especially to experience this heavenly partnership.

Cheeses that work best with white wine

- Goats' cheese is the white wine cheese par excellence whether it's a few days old, a week old or a month old (the latter can be interesting with older white wines). Sauvignon Blanc is the classic pairing but dry Riesling works well too
- Feta and other white crumbly cheeses, such as Caerphilly and Wensleydale, also work well with crisp, fruity whites
- Alpine cheeses, such as Gruyère, Comté and Beaufort, and French tomme and Italian toma cheeses all suit white wines better than red. Smooth, dry whites with good acidity work well here, as do slightly aromatic whites, such as Alsatian Pinot Gris
- Mild to medium-matured washed-rind cheeses suit aromatic wines, such as Pinot Gris and Gewurztraminer. More pungent examples are better with fortified wines or stronger drinks

Cheeses to avoid with white wine

- Blue cheeses are not good with sharply flavoured dry white wines. They don't do many favours to aged cheeses, such as Parmigiano-Reggiano, either

White wines that work best with cheese

- Smooth dry whites, such as unoaked Chardonnay and Pinot Blanc work well with egg dishes that contain cheese, such as omelette and quiche

- Crisp, 'neutral' dry whites with good acidity, such as Pinot Grigio and other dry Italian whites and the Spanish grape variety Xarel-lo, are good with salads or antipasti with cheese and mild crumbly white British cheeses like Caerphilly
- Dry whites from Switzerland and the Savoie region of France work well with Alpine cheeses and cheese fondues
- Fruity dry whites, such as Sauvignon Blanc and Greek Assyrtiko, work with goats' cheese or Greek cheeses like Feta and Halloumi
- Aromatic off-dry whites, such as Pinot Gris and Gewurztraminer, pair well with washed-rind cheeses, such as Munster
- Dry Alsace and German Rieslings are a good alternative to Sauvignon Blanc with goats' cheese
- White Bordeaux can be a fine match for an old Comté, while a barrel-fermented Chardonnay is a surprisingly good match for a full-flavoured Cheddar if you don't want to drink a port or a beer
- Southern French blends of Roussanne, Marsanne and Viognier are a good alternative to reds with sheeps' cheeses, such as Manchego

Cool, not freezing cold

We tend to think that all whites should be served well chilled but sometimes you can overdo it, particularly with more full-bodied or older whites whose opulent flavours can be dumbed down by being served too cold. While you can serve unoaked or aromatic whites like Riesling or Sauvignon Blanc at 8–10˚C or after 2 hours in the fridge, fuller whites benefit from being served at 12–14˚C or chilled for 1 hour 15 minutes–1 hour 30 minutes.

Rosé and Cheese

Now that rosé is so popular, it's more than likely you will find yourself drinking it with cheese but it won't go with everything. Light, dry rosés such as Provençal rosés will go with the same sort of cheese – particularly goats' cheese – as a fruity white. A full-bodied, ultra-ripe Cabernet or Syrah rosé will behave more like a red, although you may find them more forgiving because of their fruitiness and absence of harsh tannins.

Cheeses that go well with rosé include those that you might pair with berry-flavoured drinks, particularly milder Brie- and Camembert-style cheeses, mild cheeses, such as Chaource, and creamy cheeses, such as Finn or Explorateur. Strong, dry rosés, such as those you find in Spain and southern France, are good with sheeps' cheeses. Rosés are less successful with washed-rind and blue cheeses.

Champagne and Cheese

It might surprise you to discover that Champagne can be excellent with cheese, and not just cheese canapés, whose 'umami' (savoury) flavours blend beautifully with the biscuity flavour of a mature sparkling wine. Champagne also works well with a slightly chalky cheese, such as a Chaource (a classic match), a delicately flavoured young goats' cheese, or a double- or triple-crème cheese. If you're lucky enough to have a vintage Champagne on your hands, it will be sensational with an aged Parmigiano-Reggiano or a Vacherin Mont d'Or. For a Valentine's treat, try serving a truffle-infused cheese, such as a Caprini Tartufo, or a heart-shaped Cœur de Neufchâtel with a rosé Champagne – a wonderful way to woo any cheese-lover!

Sweet Wine and Cheese

Why do sweet wines go so extraordinarily well withcheese? It's not just blues (although they are the outstanding match) but hard cheeses and washed-rinded cheeses too. A superb Sauternes will shine with almost every cheese you put with it.

Certainly the lusciousness of many sweet wines helps to make them shine: it coats the palate with syrupy sweetness and diminishes the effect of any bitterness in the cheese. Many have fruit flavours that are naturally complementary to cheese, such as grapes, peach, apricot and quince or, in the case of sweet red wines, plum and blackberries. And some have a crisp acidity that helps to counterbalance the semi-soft texture of washed-rind cheeses that can so easily defeat a red.

There's still a residual feeling that sweet wines are not somehow serious, or that they are a needless indulgence at the end of a long meal, but do give them a try before you rule them out – your guests are sure to be impressed!

Cheeses that work best with sweet wines

- Any blue cheese, whether it's crumbly like Stilton or Fourme d'Ambert, creamy like Gorgonzola or salty like Roquefort, will find a sweet wine partner
- Powerful washed-rind cheeses, such as Epoisses or Munster, work just as well with a sweet wine as they do with an aromatic one like Gewurztraminer. Try them with a wine that's both sweet and aromatic, such as a vendange tardive (a late-harvest sweet wine) or a late-harvest Gewurztraminer, and the effect should be sensational!
- Sheep's cheeses can be highly enjoyable with sweet wine. Try an Ossau-Iraty-Brebis with a Jurançon or Pacherenc du Vic-Bilh from the south-west of France
- Aged Parmigiano-Reggiano and Gouda are delicious with a sweet red wine like Banyuls or Maury
- Cheddar is good with port but also works amazingly well with sweet wines like Sauternes

Cheeses to avoid with sweet wine

There are better things than sweet wine to drink with fresh young goats' cheeses and delicately flavoured cheeses, such as Chaource. Sweet wines also tend to dominate milder English regional cheese, such as Caerphilly, Cheshire and Wensleydale.

Sweet wines that work best with cheese

- Sauternes and similar sweet wines from the Bordeaux region, like late-harvest Sauvignon Blancs. The classic pairing is Roquefort, but they go with a much wider range of blues – and other cheeses
- Richly flavoured sweet wines, such as Tokaji from Hungary, Vin Santo and the exotic Passito di Pantelleria from the tiny island just off the Sicilian coast. Again, they are great partners for a blue cheese but a good companion for a carefully chosen cheese board or plate that includes strongly flavoured cheeses
- Sweet red wines, such as Banyuls, Maury and Recioto are interesting substitutes for port (see page 46) with blue cheese but they are also good with sheep's cheeses and aged cheeses, such as Parmigiano-Reggiano and Mimolette
- Other sweet wines, such as southern French, Greek and Spanish Muscat, will do a good job. You can also find some spectacular matches for aged Alsace, Austrian or German Riesling although they do less well across the board. Matured goats' cheese, Alpine cheese and hard sheeps' cheese work best

Add a luscious fruit

A good tip when you are pairing food and wine is to introduce an ingredient that will create a link or 'bridge' between the two, complementing the food and picking out flavours in the wine. With sweet wines and cheese, that could be a ripe peach or nectarine with a Sauternes, a few dried apricots (or nuts) with a Tokaji or a cherry compote with a sweet red wine like port.

Port, sherry and other fortified wines and cheese

Port is so firmly associated with cheese that other fortified wines don't get a look-in, but sherry, Madeira and similar wines can be just as successful. People can be a little reluctant to bring out a strong wine at the end of dinner, so you could offer these pairings as an aperitif or an imaginative, between-meals snack – a late afternoon alternative to tea or even an indulgent mid-morning offering for weekend guests if lunch is running late! A small glass of port or sherry and a nibble of cheese also make a nice nightcap if you've eaten early (but not too much of either, or you may have a sleepless night!).

Cheeses that work best with Dry, tangy wines (Fino and Manzanilla Sherry and Sercial Madeira)

- Hard Spanish and Basque sheeps' cheeses, such as Manchego and Ossau-Iraty (especially with accompanying green olives and almonds)
- Aged goats' cheeses

Dry, tangy wines are less good with rich, creamy cheeses.

Cheeses that work best with Dry, nutty wines (dry Amontillado, Palo Cortado and dry Oloroso sherries, Verdelho Madeira and 20-year-old Tawny Port)

- Hard Swiss-style cheeses, such as cave-aged Gruyère, Beaufort and Comté, Cheddar, Red Leicester
- Gouda-style cheeses, mature Parmigiano-Reggiano and Sbrinz

Less good with with young, moussey goats' cheeses.

Cheeses that work best with Pale, sweet wines (Cream Sherries and White Port)

- Mild blues, such as Gorgonzola dolce (Dolcelatte), Cambozola and other blue Brie
- Mild, hard sheeps' cheeses

Pale, sweet wines tend to work less well with mature Cheddar and strong blue cheeses.

Cheeses that work best with Sweet, nutty wines (10-year-old and some 20-year-old Tawny Ports)

- Mellow blues, such as Stilton
- Medium-matured Cheddar and Gouda-style cheeses, Mimolette
- Milder washed-rind cheeses

Sweet, nutty wines are less good with young goats' cheeses, Feta and other crumbly white cheeses.

Cheeses that work best with plum- and berry-flavoured wines (late-bottled Vintage and Vintage Port)

- Blue cheeses, especially Stilton
- Cheddar

These wines tend to be less good with young goats' cheeses but overall are a pretty versatile all-rounder.

Cheeses that work best with Sweet, raisiny wines (Sweet Oloroso and Pedro Ximenez sherries, and Bual and Malmsey Madeiras)

- Tangy Cheddar and strong blues, such as Roquefort and Cabrales, especially with raisins, figs or dates

Raisiny, sweet wines don't work so well with young goats' cheeses, Brie, Camembert and garlic-flavoured cheeses.

CHEESE TIPS:

You can enhance a match between cheese and a fortified wine by bringing in accompaniments that reflect the flavours in the wine: olives and almonds in the case of a fino sherry; raisins, dried figs, dates or ready-to-eat prunes with stronger, sweeter sherries; a damson or cherry compote with a brambly, late-vintage port..

Seasonal Cheeseboards

Wine and cheese is supposed to be the perfect match, but how often have you been disappointed at the combination? Your favourite red wine may taste great with one or two of the cheeses on the board, but clash horribly with another. Or you may find that a delicate cheese may be totally overwhelmed by the wine.

It's time we changed the way we think about cheeseboards, designing them, like other foods we serve, to reflect the seasons and our mood. This is an approach that makes abundant sense, as so many cheeses themselves are seasonal. Why would you want to serve the same cheeseboard in June as in December?

It also helps to limit the number of cheeses you serve and pick them carefully. If you include a strong, stinky French cheese and a pungent blue in your selection, for example, you'll struggle to find a wine to go with them both. The traditional approach is to serve the widest range of cheeses you can afford, displaying your generosity as a host, but the chances are that your guests will enjoy the experience just as much if you select two or three that work perfectly together.

You can also be imaginative in the way you dress your cheeseboard, introducing accompaniments that will complement the flavour of your cheeses and reflect the time of year. Warm, rich dried fruits, for example, in winter when fresh fruits are less widely available; and tender, fresh young salad leaves in springtime.

Spring

Spring and early summer is the ideal time of year to enjoy fresh young goats' cheeses and their perfect partner, Sauvignon Blanc. Choose two or three cheeses for contrast: one young, light and moussey, one that has been matured a little longer and one that has been rolled in herbs. Serve them with a lightly dressed herb salad. You could also add a wedge of tangy Italian pecorino and a few shelled broad/fava beans – a delicious combination. Breads should be light too – ciabatta and some crisp Italian flatbread. A good choice of Sauvignon would be a Sancerre or Pouilly Fumé, but choose any unoaked Sauvignon that you enjoy.

Summer

In summertime the flavours tend to be richer and fuller, begging for a full-bodied red wine. The type of cheese that works best are the smooth, tangy hard sheeps' cheeses you traditionally find in Spain and the Basque region of France – full flavoured, but without any touch of bitterness. You could also add a Fleur de Maquis, a Corsican cheese rolled in rosemary and fennel. Include some other Mediterranean ingredients – a few chewy sun-dried tomatoes, some olives and olive bread – and you've got the perfect foil for a rich southern French red from the Languedoc or the Rhône, or a Spanish red like a Rioja.

Autumn

The ploughman's lunch re-invented. Forget wine for once and turn to cider, the natural accompaniment for autumn fruits and flavours. Mix and match among ancient and modern British and Irish cheeses – a fine Cheddar, an Irish Adrahan or other washed-rind cheese, a snowy white-rinded Tunworth and maybe even a mellow blue. Serve with fine, flavourful eating apples and pears, a mild apple chutney (homemade or bought) and an old-fashioned white crusty loaf, and pour chunky glasses of cool, artisanal cider, offering your guests a choice of dry or medium-dry if you wish. You could even offer brandy glasses of Somerset Cider Brandy or Calvados to round off the meal.

Winter

Port and blue cheese is a classic pairing, but give it a modern twist. Serve three contrasting cheeses, say a Stilton, a Roquefort and a mild Gorgonzola or Harbourne Blue (a mild blue goats' cheese from Devon) and serve them with a collection of dried fruits such as Medjool dates, figs or raisins and a handful of walnuts and brazil nuts. Echo the dried fruit flavours with a raisin and rosemary bread or a walnut bread, and introduce a little crunch with oat biscuits or oatcakes. This is the perfect occasion to bring out a vintage port (which you'll need to decant) or a fine Sauternes or a Tokay from Hungary. What blue cheeses need is sweetness.

Wine and cheese 'flights'

A brilliant idea for wine and cheese lovers pioneered by the innovative Artisanal cheese shop and bistro in New York, is to arrange a wine and cheese 'flight'.

Cheese and sherry flight, from left: Oude Gouda and dry oloroso, Gorgonzola and cream sherry, Manchego and fino

This is a selection of three different wines and cheeses served in small quantities to taste and compare. Usually the wines will be of a similar type, for example three or four wines made from the same grape – say Syrah or Shiraz – or four wines of different types from the same wine region, say the Loire. The idea applies equally well to other drinks. Why not try a sherry and cheese flight, a whisky and cheese flight or even an apple-flavoured drinks and cheese flight, with a selection including cider, Calvados and Pommeau.

Cheese and Wine Parties

It must be at least 40 years ago now that cheese and wine parties were all the rage. You can see why – they were a simple way to entertain. No cooking, just a bit of cutting up. And the cheese was so bland that by and large there was never any problem serving red wine. Maybe it's time to revisit these parties now that the range of high-quality cheeses open to us is greater than ever before. But let's update them and give them a stylish spin. Here are a few suggestions that are sure to impress your guests.

Cheese and wine 'stations'

This is a great way to enjoy wine and cheese together and learn a little in the process. Set up four to six tables around the room, depending how much room you have, each with a different style of cheese and a different wine and some accompanying biscuits and/or bread. They could include:

- A goats' cheese with Sauvignon Blanc (it's always good to have at least a couple of goats' cheeses as an option for those who are intolerant to cows' milk)
- A Brie- or Camembert-style cheese with a fruity Beaujolais or Pinot Noir
- A Cheddar with an oaked Chardonnay and a Merlot (it will be interesting for your guests to see how the two compare)
- A hard sheep's cheese with a Rioja or other Tempranillo-based red
- A washed-rind cheese, such as Munster with a Gewurztraminer
- A blue cheese with port. You could, of course, carry out a similar exercise with different beers and cheeses. Or surprise guests with an apple-flavoured drinks and cheese evening.

Cheese and champagne party

It doesn't have to be Champagne – a cheaper kind of fizz would be fine – but sparkling wine does go surprisingly well with cheese, particularly cheese pastries and biscuits.

You could lay on a range of different canapés, such as gougères, parmesan biscuits or other little crisp cheese biscuits or tartlets made with cheese pastry; individual quiches or mini cheese muffin; crostini topped with cheese; and mini-sandwiches or blinis topped with cream cheese and smoked salmon. (There is no reason why you should make all these yourself. You can buy excellent cheese biscuits these days, for example.)

A cheese and wine-themed dinner party

Your guests will be amazed at how different each course will taste. For a dinner party spin on the traditional cheese and wine party kick off with one of the nibbles suggested above, then you could serve the Parmesan Custards (see page 59) or the Stichelton and Steak Winter Salad (also on page 59) as a starter, followed by a main course of steak with balsamic onions and molten blue cheese or roast lamb with a side dish of Mushroom Dauphinois (see page 60) and finish off the meal with the Lemon and Blueberry Upside-down Cheesecakes (see page 63), pairing each course with a matching wine – refer to the suggestions under individual recipes.

A casual mac 'n' cheese 'n' wine supper

For a fun and frugal evening supper party with a big group of friends, serve a classic macaroni cheese (try making a large batch of the recipe given on page 60) and pair it with a choice of both red and white wine.

Round-the-world cheese

For an internationally themed cheese and wine party, choose a country (or even a selection of countries) and serve their classic cheeses along with wines from the same local origin and local accompaniments. Here are some ideas to get you started, but the possibilities are endless.

Cheese tapas

This is one of the easiest themes to organize since tapas ingredients are so widely available. A very simple get-together for a drink could involve some fine slices of Manchego with membrillo (quince paste), sliced chorizo, Marcona almonds and green olives with glasses of fresh manzanilla sherry (see picture opposite).

For a more substantial meal, you could add a tortilla, red peppers stuffed with goats' cheese or some croquetas (crisp little deep-fried rissoles with a creamy, cheesy filling). There are also other interesting Spanish cheeses to explore, including Majorero from the Canary Islands, and two powerful blues, Valdeón and Cabrales, which you could pair with sweet sherry and raisins.

Cheese antipasti

Again, this is a very simple way of entertaining at short notice. A selection of preserved grilled vegetables, such as artichokes, mushrooms and peppers, with Parma or San Daniele ham, Mozzarella balls, ciabatta and breadsticks makes a delicious, impromptu feast (see above left). Serve with a crisp, dry Italian white, such as Pinot Grigio from the Alto Adige, a Prosecco or a lightly chilled Valpolicella.

If you wanted to add a couple of hot dishes, you could serve some arancini (deep-fried risotto balls) and pizzette (mini-pizzas) or, of course, go on to a pasta course.

A late-night French bistro supper

Follow the example of Parisian party-goers who used to go to Les Halles in the early hours of the morning for sustaining bowlfuls of onion soup, topped with slices of grilled country bread and melted cheese. It's a great finale to an evening at the theatre or a chilly outdoor sporting event. A simple dry white wine (Aligoté is the traditional choice), some crusty bread and a leafy green salad make perfect accompaniments. Finish the meal off with a classic French fruit tart.

Cooking with Cheese

Perfect for pairing with wine, the delicious recipes on the following pages provide both classic and original ideas for cooking with cheese – and will befit a variety of occasions. Follow the suggestions on page 53 for a cheese and wine-themed dinner party, or simply prepare any of these dishes for a casual weekend supper. To get the most out of the dishes, see the tip boxes for ideas of what to drink alongside

Leek and blue cheese quiche with hazelnut pastry

A good home-made quiche is a wonderful way to enjoy cheese. You can always use ready-made pastry to save time but this nutty pastry does have a great flavour. If you don't like blue cheese you could easily substitute Cheddar, Gouda or any other full-flavoured cheese. Do buy leeks that still have their green leaves rather than ready-trimmed ones.

3 leeks (about 400 g/14 oz. untrimmed)

40 g/3 tablespoons butter

3 large eggs

250 ml/1 cup whipping cream

30 g/¹⁄₃ cup grated mature Parmesan cheese

100 g/3½ oz. medium-strong blue cheese, e.g. Stilton, crumbled

sea salt and freshly ground black pepper

For the hazelnut pastry:

25 g/2 tablespoons whole shelled hazelnuts

75 g/²⁄₃ cup plain/all-purpose flour

50 g/¹⁄₃ cup wholemeal/whole-wheat flour

75 g/5 tablespoons chilled butter, cubed

3–4 tablespoons iced water

a deep 23-cm/9-inch loose-based quiche pan baking beans

Serves 4–6

Preheat the oven to 190°C (375°F) Gas 5.

First make the pastry. Put the hazelnuts on a baking sheet and roast in the preheated oven for 10 minutes or until the skins turn dark brown. (Turn off the oven.) Leave to cool for a few minutes, then tip them onto a clean dish towel and rub off the skins. Transfer to a food processor and pulse until finely chopped but not powdery, then add the flours and pulse once or twice to mix. Add the butter and pulse to incorporate, then add just enough of the iced water to bring the mixture together. Pat the pastry into a ball, wrap in clingfilm/plastic wrap and leave to rest in the fridge for 1 hour.

Meanwhile, trim the bases and cut the coarse outer leaves from the leeks. Thinly slice the leeks and rinse thoroughly to get rid of any dirt or grit. Heat the butter in a large frying pan and fry the leeks for 5–6 minutes until beginning to soften. Season well and set aside to cool.

Roll the pastry out to a circle big enough to fit your quiche pan. Carefully lower the pastry into the pan, pressing it into the edges, and lightly prick the base with a fork. Leave any overhanging pastry untrimmed. Refrigerate for 20 minutes. Preheat the oven again to 190°C (375°F) Gas 5.

Line the pastry case with baking paper, fill with baking beans and bake in the preheated oven for about 12 minutes. Leave the oven on.

Separate 1 of the eggs, reserve the white and beat the yolk and the other 2 whole eggs together. Measure the cream into a jug/pitcher, add the beaten egg and half the Parmesan, season with pepper and beat well.

Remove the paper and beans from the pastry case and brush lightly with the reserved egg white. Return to the oven for another 5 minutes, then remove from the oven and reduce the oven temperature to 180°C (350°F) Gas 4. Trim the overhanging edge of pastry with a sharp knife. Scatter half the blue cheese in the pastry case, spoon over the leeks, then cover with the remaining blue cheese. Carefully pour the egg and cream mixture evenly over the top (only use as much as you need to fill the case). Sprinkle over the remaining Parmesan. Bake for about 35–40 minutes until the top is puffed up and lightly browned. Leave to cool for about 20 minutes before serving. (I personally think it's nicest at room temperature.)

WINE RECOMMENDATION:

A smooth dry white wine like a Pinot Blanc, a subtly oaked Chardonnay, or a Chenin Blanc. Or you could opt for a cider, which is always good with leeks.

Stichelton and steak winter salad

Stichelton is a wonderful new unpasteurized blue which is made to a similar recipe to Stilton (which you can easily substitute). A very easy and stylish dinner for two.

250 g/9 oz. lean steak, trimmed of any fat

extra virgin olive oil

1 onion, thinly sliced

about 1 tablespoon balsamic vinegar

75 g/½ cup cherry tomatoes

2 handfuls rocket/arugula

60 g/2 oz. Stichelton or Stilton, rind removed

sea salt and freshly ground black pepper

Serves 2

Lay the steak on a sheet of baking paper on a chopping board, cover with another sheet of baking paper and beat out with a meat mallet or rolling pin. Rub a little olive oil into both sides of the steak and season lightly with salt and pepper. Heat a ridged griddle pan until almost smoking, then lay the steak in the pan and cook for 1 minute. Turn and cook for 1 minute on the other side, then transfer from the pan to a plate.

Turn down the heat under the pan slightly, smear a little oil over the onion slices and place them in a single layer in the pan. Cook for a couple of minutes until beginning to turn dark brown, then carefully turn and cook the other side. Set aside on another plate and drizzle over a little of the balsamic vinegar.

Finally, tip the cherry tomatoes into the pan with a little extra oil, if necessary, and roll them around until the skins begin to burst.

Cut the steak into fine slices with a sharp knife. Divide the rocket/arugula between 2 plates, top with the onions and arrange the tomatoes round the plate. Scatter over the steak slices and crumble over the Stichelton. Trickle over a little extra oil and balsamic vinegar and season with pepper. This salad is good with a crusty baguette, warm ciabatta or a baked potato.

Parmesan custards with anchovy toasts

This delectable starter is the inspiration of Rowley Leigh who added it to the menu of his London restaurant, Le Café Anglais.

300 ml/1¼ cups single/light cream

300 ml/1¼ cups whole milk

100 g/1 cup finely grated Parmesan

4 egg yolks

cayenne pepper

12 anchovy fillets

50 g/3 tablespoons unsalted butter

8 very thin slices of pain de campagne/rustic loaf

sea salt and finely ground white pepper

8 x 80-ml/⅓-cup ramekins or ovenproof dishes, buttered

Serves 8

Mix the cream, milk and all but 1 tablespoon of the Parmesan in a heatproof bowl, place it over a saucepan of boiling water and warm it gently until the Parmesan has melted. Remove the bowl from on top of the pan and leave to cool completely. Preheat the oven to 150°C (300°F) Gas 2.

Whisk the egg yolks, a pinch of salt, a pinch of white pepper and a little cayenne pepper into the cool cream mixture, then pour into the prepared ramekins. Place the ramekins in an ovenproof dish in the oven, then pour boiling water from the kettle into the dish to reach halfway up the ramekins. Cover the whole dish with a sheet of buttered baking paper and bake in the preheated oven for 15 minutes or until the custards have just set. Remove from the oven and turn on the grill/broiler.

Mash the anchovies and butter to make a smooth paste and spread over 4 of the slices of bread. Cover with the remaining bread and toast in a sandwich maker or panini machine. Sprinkle the remaining Parmesan over the warm custards and brown gently under the hot grill/broiler. Cut the toasted anchovy sandwiches into fingers and serve alongside the custards.

WINE RECOMMENDATION:

You might be surprised, given that red wine and blue cheese aren't generally the most accommodating of partners, but a fruity Cabernet Sauvignon will go well with this. The steak and onions counteract the slight bitterness of the cheese.

WINE RECOMMENDATION:

Champagne is a great pairing with Parmesan but you could serve any similar dry sparkling wine.

Mushroom Dauphinois

Adding mushrooms and extra cheese to this gorgeously creamy French potato classic makes it substantial enough to serve on its own, as well as being the perfect accompaniment for roast lamb.

40 g/3 tablespoons butter, cubed, plus a little extra for the topping
250 g/9 oz. chestnut/cremini mushrooms, trimmed and sliced
1 teaspoon finely chopped fresh thyme leaves (optional)
300 ml/1¼ cups whipping cream
2 garlic cloves, thinly sliced
600 g/1¼ lbs. waxy potatoes, e.g. Desirée
50 g/½ cup finely grated Gruyère, Beaufort or Comté
15 g/2 tablespoons freshly grated Parmesan
sea salt and freshly ground black pepper

a shallow ovenproof dish, buttered

Serves 6

Preheat the oven to 190°C (375°F) Gas 5.

Heat a large frying pan or wok and add the butter. When it has melted and stopped foaming, tip in the mushrooms. Fry for a couple of minutes, then stir-fry until lightly browned. Stir in the thyme and remove from the heat.

Pour the cream into a small saucepan and heat very gently with the garlic. Turn off the heat and leave to infuse while you peel the potatoes and cut them into very thin slices.

Arrange a layer of potatoes over the bottom of the prepared ovenproof dish. Tip half the mushrooms over the potatoes, sprinkle over half the Gruyère and season with salt and pepper. Put another layer of potatoes on top, then the remaining mushrooms and Gruyère and season again. Top with the remaining potatoes. Carefully pour over the infused cream, distributing it evenly over the dish. Sprinkle the top with Parmesan. Chop a small slice of butter into little pieces and dot over the top. Bake in the preheated oven for 1 hour–1 hour 15 minutes until the top is browned and the potatoes thoroughly cooked. Leave to rest for at least 5 minutes before serving.

WINE RECOMMENDATION:
Most medium-bodied reds would work well with this – Pinot Noir would be particularly delicious.

Mac 'n' Greens

A healthy spin on macaroni cheese which can be used as a side for a roast or grilled meat.

50 g/3 tablespoons butter
1 medium/large leek, trimmed and thinly sliced
40 g/⅓ cup plain/all-purpose flour
600 ml/2½ cups semi-skimmed milk
a head of broccoli divided into small florets (about 300 g/10 oz. florets)
350 g/12 oz. penne (plain or wholewheat)

2 handfuls of chard or spinach leaves
150 g/5½ oz. mature Gruyère
3 generous tablespoons freshly grated Parmesan
sea salt, freshly ground black pepper and grated nutmeg

4 or 6 individual ovenproof dishes, lightly buttered

Serves 4 as a main course or 6 as a side

Put the butter in a medium non-stick saucepan and melt gently. Add the leeks, stir and cook for 1 minute, then stir in the flour and cook for a few seconds. Take the pan off the heat and gradually add the milk, stirring continuously. Put the pan back on the hob, increase the heat slightly, then bring the milk gradually up to simmering point. Turn the heat right down again and leave the sauce over very low heat.

Fill a large saucepan with boiling water from the kettle, bring back to the boil, add salt, then add the broccoli and blanch for a couple of minutes. Transfer the broccoli to a sieve/strainer with a slotted spoon and rinse with cold water. Tip the pasta into the same water in the pan and cook for the time recommended on the pack.

Wash and remove the stalk and central rib from the chard or spinach (unless using baby leaves). Just before the pasta is ready, stir half the Gruyère and the Parmesan into the sauce and check the seasoning, adding salt, pepper, nutmeg and more Parmesan, if necessary. Add the broccoli and chard or spinach, stir and set aside for 3–4 minutes. Preheat the grill/broiler.

Drain the pasta and divide between the prepared ovenproof dishes. Pour over the sauce and vegetables and mix gently, then sprinkle over the remaining Gruyère. Place the dishes on a baking sheet and grill/broil for 5 minutes until the cheese is brown and bubbling.

WINE RECOMMENDATION:
If you're making this as a side for grilled pork or veal, serve a medium-bodied Italian red. An unoaked Chardonnay or Italian white like a Soave would work well with it on its own.

Warm pear, gorgonzola and pecan tartlets with maple drizzle

A cheese course and dessert rolled into one – a fabulous finale for a dinner party.

375 g/13 oz. ready-rolled puff pastry, thawed if frozen
1 egg, lightly beaten
200 g/7 oz. Gorgonzola
4 tablespoons double/heavy cream
75 g/½ cup shelled pecan nuts or walnuts
2–3 ripe pears
2 tablespoons maple syrup
cayenne pepper

Serves 6

Preheat the oven to 220°C (425°F) Gas 7.

Take the pastry out of the fridge and leave to warm up a little for 10–15 minutes.

Unroll the pastry, cut it in half horizontally, then cut each of the halves into 3 to make 6 equal-sized pieces. With the tip of a sharp knife, score round each of the squares about 1.5 cm/½ inch from the edge to make a border. Lightly brush the border with beaten egg, taking care not to brush over the cut you've made (otherwise the pastry won't puff up around the edge of the tartlets).

Put the Gorgonzola in a bowl and break up roughly with a fork, then stir in the cream. Season with a little cayenne pepper and spread over the bases of the tartlets, taking care not to cover the border. Roughly break up the pecan nuts and divide between the tartlets. Peel, core and quarter the pears, cut each quarter into 3 wedges and lay them in overlapping slices on top of the cheese and nuts. Drizzle a teaspoonful of maple syrup over each tart and bake in the preheated oven for 15–20 minutes until the pastry is well browned and puffed up. Leave to cool for 5 minutes before serving.

WINE RECOMMENDATION:
A glass of lightly chilled young tawny port or an Australian Liqueur Muscat would be delicious with these.

Lemon and blueberry upside-down cheesecakes

A gorgeous sweet, lemony version of the fashionable French verrine and really easy to make.

110 g/4 oz. digestive biscuits/graham crackers
55 g/4 tablespoons butter
1 teaspoon ground cinnamon
250 g/9 oz. mascarpone
3–4 tablespoons home-made or good-quality shop-bought lemon curd
2–3 tablespoons semi-skimmed milk
2–3 teaspoons freshly squeezed lemon juice, strained
250 g/2 cups fresh or frozen blueberries

4–6 small tumblers

Serves 4–6

Preheat the oven to 190°C (375°F) Gas 5.

Put the biscuits/crackers in a plastic bag and crush with a rolling pin until you have even-sized crumbs. (You can do this in a food processor but it tends to make them a bit fine and powdery.) Melt the butter in a small saucepan, stir in the cinnamon, cook for a few seconds, then stir in the crumbs until they have absorbed all the butter. Tip into a baking pan and and bake in the preheated oven for 5 minutes until the crumbs are crisp. Set aside to cool.

Tip the mascarpone into a bowl and mix in the lemon curd with a wooden spoon until smooth. (Don't use an electric beater – it will make the mixture seize up and become too buttery.) Add the milk to give a softer, more spoonable consistency and a little lemon juice to adjust the sweetness.

Divide the blueberries between the tumblers. Spoon over the mascarpone mixture and top with the baked crumbs. Cover the glasses with clingfilm/plastic wrap and refrigerate for an hour or so. (The bases can be made further in advance but don't add the crumble topping too far ahead otherwise it will go soggy.)

• You can vary this idea with other curds and fruits. A raspberry curd and mascarpone mixture, for example, would be delicious with fresh raspberries underneath; a lime curd with chopped kiwi fruit; or an orange curd with mandarin oranges.

WINE RECOMMENDATION:
A late-harvest, Beerenauslese or vendange tardive Riesling would go well with this.

Summer Menus

An Italian Al Fresco Lunch

Ham and melon platter • Tuscan-style roast veal with wild mushrooms • Roast new potatoes with olive oil • Buttered spinach • Grape and lemon mascarpone tart

A Provençal-style Lunch

Anchovy and green olive dip • Ciabatta toasts • Mini pissaladières • Seared tuna with tomatoes and gremolata • Apricot tart with Muscat de Beaumes-de-Venise

A Summer Picnic

Sun-dried tomato, olive and basil bread • Chicken tonnato pasta salad Lavender shortbread • Homemade lemonade

A Seafood Lunch

Seafood jellies with white wine and dill • Sicilian-spiced seabass with grilled tomatoes and baby fennel • Strawberry tiramisù

An Around-the-World Barbecue

Pork and olive empanadas • Cheese empanadas • Gazpacho shots • Butterflied leg of lamb with cumin, lemon and garlic • Kisir • Sparkling Shiraz and summer berry jellies • Sparkling nectarine and blueberry jellies • Exotic Sea Breeze Watermelon and strawberry cooler

Cooling Food for a Hot Evening

Spiced mango, carrot and chilli soup • Thai-style beef with tomato and herb salad Prawn and cucumber sesame noodles • Piña Colada sherbet • Exotic fruits

An Italian Al Fresco Lunch

Combine an Italian menu with eating out of doors, and you have a guaranteed formula for happy guests. The Ham and Melon Platter couldn't be simpler to put together and, with its pale green, orange and pink colours, makes a strikingly pretty plate to bring to the table. The Grape and Lemon Mascarpone Tart takes very little time to assemble – so all you have to do is keep an eye on your typically Tuscan-style roast. You can keep the Italian theme going with the drinks you serve.

Ham and melon platter

*

*Tuscan-style roast veal
with wild mushrooms*
Roast new potatoes with olive oil
Buttered spinach

*

Grape and lemon mascarpone tart

*

To Drink

The charming Venetian wine Prosecco makes a perfect aperitivo – mix it with freshly pressed peach juice for a classic Bellini cocktail. Serve a Cinzano Bianco and soda with the Ham and Melon platter and accompany the veal with an elegant Chianti Classico Riserva. The fragrant summer tart perfectly suits a glass of honeysuckle sweet Moscato d'Asti, served well chilled in Champagne flutes.

Ham and melon platter

On lazy summer days, this mouthwatering, easy-to-assemble starter is the perfect way to kick off a relaxed lunch.

For colour contrast you need an orange Canteloupe or Charentais melon and a green Galia, Ogen or Honeydew melon, and some thinly sliced Parma ham and prosciutto cotto all'erbe. Quarter and deseed the melons, cut the wedges off the skin, then cut them into thick slices. Arrange on a big plate along with loosely draped slices of ham. The platter wants to look quite casual – lavish and generous, rather than arranged into perfectly regimented rows. Serve with some olive breadsticks and mini ciabattas, refreshed in the oven.

WINE RECOMMENDATION:

Forgo wine here and serve a Cinzano Bianco and soda with the ham and melon platter, as its sweetness and delicate herbal notes will be a perfect match.

Tuscan-style roast veal with wild mushrooms

This light but intensely flavourful dish is brilliant for matching with wine – the perfect partner for a Chianti Classico Riserva. You can also prepare the roast with a rolled loin or rack of pork, if preferred.

1 kg/2¼ lb. boned, rolled loin or rack of veal or pork (including the bones)

3 tablespoons olive oil

50 g/3 tablespoons butter

1 onion, cut into 8

1 large carrot, cut into chunks

3 large garlic cloves, peeled and quartered

3 sprigs of rosemary

250 ml/1 cup dry Italian white wine

250 ml/1 cup fresh chicken stock or light vegetable stock made with ½ organic stock cube

150 g/5 oz. wild mushrooms

2 teaspoons plain/all-purpose flour

a few drops of Marsala or sweet sherry (optional)

sea salt and freshly ground black pepper

a large, deep, lidded and flameproof casserole

Serves 6

Preheat the oven to 200°C (400°F) Gas 6. Pat the veal dry and season all over with salt and pepper. Put the casserole over medium heat, add 1½ tablespoons of the olive oil, heat for a minute, then add 15 g/1 tablespoon of the butter. When the foaming dies down, put in the veal, bones, onion and carrot and brown on all sides, turning regularly.

Add the garlic and rosemary to the casserole, stir and add 3 tablespoons of the white wine. Cover with a lid and transfer to the oven. Roast for about 2 hours. Check occasionally that the meat and vegetables aren't burning and add a little more white wine if necessary.

Remove the veal from the casserole and set aside on a warmed carving plate. Cover lightly with foil and leave to rest for at least half an hour.

Pour off any surface fat from the juices in the casserole, then add the remaining white wine and bring to the boil, working in the tasty caramelized juices stuck on the side of the casserole. Simmer and reduce the liquid by half, then add half the stock and simmer for another 10 minutes. Strain through a fine mesh sieve/strainer.

Heat the remaining butter in a frying pan and fry the mushrooms until the butter and any liquid have almost evaporated. Stir in the flour. Pour in the strained stock, bring to the boil and simmer for 5 minutes. Add a little more stock if the sauce seems too thick. Check the seasoning, add salt and pepper to taste and a dash of Marsala if you like a touch of sweetness.

For a rack of veal, offer the sauce separately, otherwise finely slice the meat, arrange on a warmed platter and spoon over the sauce. Serve with roast new potatoes and buttered spinach (see overleaf).

WINE RECOMMENDATION:

A Chianti Classico Riserva will make a perfect pairing.

Roast new potatoes with olive oil

3 tablespoons olive oil
750–800 g/1½–2 lb. baby new potatoes, washed and dried
sea salt and freshly ground black pepper

Serves 6

Preheat the oven to 200°C (400°F) Gas 6 (if not already on for the meat). Measure the oil into a shallow roasting pan, tip in the potatoes and shake the pan so that they get evenly covered with oil. Put the pan in the oven and roast for about 35–40 minutes until the potatoes are nicely browned, turning them halfway through. Season lightly with salt and pepper.

Buttered spinach

750 g/1½ lb. loose spinach leaves
2 tablespoons extra virgin olive oil
25 g/2 tablespoons butter
sea salt and freshly ground black pepper
freshly grated nutmeg, to taste

Serves 6

Tip the leaves into a sinkful of cold water and give them a good swirl. Discard any damaged leaves and remove the central tough rib from the larger leaves. Drain and pack into a large saucepan without any extra water. Put the pan over low heat, cover and leave for about 5 minutes. Turn the leaves over (the bottom leaves should have collapsed). Re-cover and cook for another 3–4 minutes until all the leaves have collapsed but are still bright green. Drain thoroughly in a colander pressing out the excess water. Return the leaves to the pan and chop roughly. Add the oil and butter and heat until the spinach is hot and the butter melted. Season to taste with salt, pepper and nutmeg.

Grape and lemon mascarpone tart

A gorgeous Italian lemon liqueur gives a sharp edge to the creamy mascarpone in this simple, delicious dessert.

230 g/8 oz. ready-rolled puff pastry, thawed if frozen
2 large eggs, separated
2 tablespoons caster/superfine sugar, plus 1 teaspoon for sprinkling
250 g/9 oz. mascarpone cheese
2½ tablespoons Limoncello (lemon liqueur)
250 g/9 oz. white seedless or halved and seeded grapes, rinsed and dried
250 g/9 oz. red seedless or halved and seeded grapes, rinsed and dried
1 teaspoon icing/confectioners' sugar

a large square or rectangular baking sheet, lightly greased

Serves 6–8

Preheat the oven to 200°C (400°F) Gas 6.

Take the pastry out of the fridge and let it rest for 20 minutes. Unroll and lift carefully onto the baking sheet. Trim around the edge to make a 28-cm/11-inch round.

Whisk the egg whites and brush a thin layer onto the pastry. Sprinkle with 1 teaspoon sugar, then use a fork to prick the pastry all over. Bake for 10–12 minutes until puffy and brown. Leave to cool while you make the topping.

Tip the mascarpone cheese into a bowl and gradually work in the Limoncello. Using an electric hand whisk, beat the egg yolks with the remaining sugar until pale, thick and creamy. Gently fold the mascarpone mixture into the eggs until thoroughly blended.

Transfer the cooled pastry base to a serving plate. Spread over the mascarpone mixture and then scatter the grapes on top to get a nice mix of colours. Sift over the icing/confectioners' sugar and serve straight away, or chill the tart for a couple of hours, then sprinkle with icing/confectioners' sugar when ready to serve.

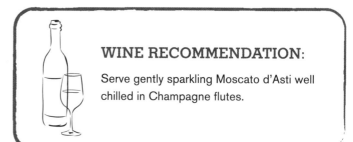

WINE RECOMMENDATION:

Serve gently sparkling Moscato d'Asti well chilled in Champagne flutes.

A Provençal-style Lunch

A light, flavourful Mediterranean lunch is perfect for summer entertaining. Start with a cool, refreshing pastis or a glass of rosé and some typically Provençal olive-based nibbles, then serve some simply seared tuna – cooked on the barbecue if you feel like firing it up. Finally, a classic apricot tart with a twist, flavoured with the gorgeous southern French dessert wine, Muscat de Beaumes-de-Venise. Simple and stylish.

Anchovy and green olive dip
Ciabatta toasts
Mini pissaladières

*

Seared tuna with tomatoes and gremolata

*

Apricot tart with Muscat de Beaumes-de-Venise

*

To Drink

Pastis is perfect to serve alongside Provençal nibbles. Or you could also start with or move on to a chilled dry rosé, which is a perfect match for the tuna. Try pairing the dessert with a Muscat de Beaumes-de-Venise to round off the meal.

Anchovy and green olive dip

This is one of the easiest dips or spreads you can make.

100-g/3½-oz. jar anchovy fillets marinated in olive oil with garlic and herbs
25 g/2 tablespoons pitted green olives
75 ml/⅓ cup Provençal or Spanish olive oil
1 tablespoon red wine vinegar
2–3 tablespoons warm water
freshly ground black pepper

50 g/¼ cup pitted green olives
3 tablespoons chopped flat leaf parsley
ciabatta toasts (below) to serve
a selection of crudités (radishes, carrot and fennel strips) to serve

Serves 6

Tip the anchovies and their oil into a food processor with the olives and whizz until smooth. Gradually add the olive oil until you have a mayonnaise-type consistency. Add the red wine vinegar and sufficient warm water to make a spreadable consistency. Season with black pepper.

Chop the remaining olives and parsley together for the topping. Spread the anchovy paste thinly over the toasts and spoon over a little of the green olive topping. Serve on a platter decorated with radishes, carrot sticks and fennel strips.

Ciabatta toasts

It's worth making a large batch of these, as they keep well.

2 ready-to-bake ciabatta loaves
olive oil spray or 4–6 tablespoons light olive oil

Makes about 30–32 slices

Preheat the oven to 180°C (350°F) Gas 4. Cut the ciabatta on the slant into fairly thin slices. Spray both sides with olive oil or pour the olive oil on the baking trays and dip the slices of ciabatta in it. Bake for 15 minutes, turning the slices halfway through. Repeat with any remaining ciabatta slices. Cool, then store the toasts in an airtight container.

WINE RECOMMENDATION:

A chilled dry rosé or a glass of pastis. Dilute pastis (try Henri Bardouin) about 1:5 with cool (not iced) water and serve in small tumblers.

Mini pissaladières

For the topping:

2 tablespoons olive oil

2 large sweet onions (about 500 g/1 lb. in total), thinly sliced

1 garlic clove, finely chopped

1 teaspoon finely chopped thyme or ½ teaspoon dried thyme

150 g/5½ oz. small pitted marinated black olives

sea salt and freshly ground black pepper

a few small basil leaves, to garnish

For the pastry:

100 g/3½ oz. Quark or cream cheese

100 g/7 tablespoons butter, at room temperature, cut into cubes

125 g/1 cup plain/all-purpose flour

1 teaspoon baking powder

a good pinch of salt

an 8-cm/3-inch pastry cutter

2 x 12-hole shallow tartlet tins

Makes about 12–14

Heat the oil in a large flameproof casserole or saucepan. Tip in the onions, then cook over a medium heat until they have begun to collapse (about 10 minutes). Stir in the garlic and thyme, turn the heat down a little and continue to cook for another 30–40 minutes until the onions are soft and golden and any liquid has evaporated, taking care that they don't catch and burn. Season with salt and pepper and set aside to cool.

While the onions are cooking, make the pastry. Tip the Quark into a food processor with the butter and process until smooth. Sift the flour with the baking powder and salt and add to the Quark and butter mixture in 2 batches, using the pulse to incorporate it. Once the mixture starts to form a ball, turn it out of the food processor onto a floured surface and form it into a flat disc. Put it in a plastic bag and leave it to chill for an hour in the fridge.

When ready to cook the tartlets, heat the oven to 220°C (425°F) Gas 7. Roll out the pastry quite thinly. Stamp rounds out of the pastry, re-rolling the offcuts as necessary, and lay them in the hollows of the tartlet tins. Spoon in teaspoonfuls of the cooled onion mixture and top with an olive. Bake for 15–20 minutes until the pastry is puffed up and golden. Cool for 10 minutes, then remove the tarts carefully from the tin and arrange on a plate. Scatter with a few small basil leaves and serve. You can bake and freeze these, then reheat them from frozen in a moderate oven.

Seared tuna with tomatoes and gremolata

This simple dish can equally well be adapted to a conventional grill/broiler or an outside grill.

2 unwaxed lemons
3 large garlic cloves
a large handful (about 40 g/1½ oz.) parsley
2 rounded tablespoons capers, rinsed if salted
6 fresh tuna steaks, about 150 g/5 oz. each
350 g/12 oz. pomodorino or other cherry tomatoes
100 g/3½ oz. wild rocket/arugula
sea salt and freshly ground black pepper
extra virgin olive oil, to drizzle

Serves 6

First make the gremolata. Grate the zest finely from the lemons, taking care not to remove too much white pith. Peel the garlic cloves and chop them finely. Take the tough ends off the parsley stalks and finely chop the leaves. Roughly chop the capers, then pull all the ingredients together on the chopping board and chop them together to mix them thoroughly. Set aside in a bowl.

When you're ready to cook, heat a ridged grill pan until it is almost smoking (about 3 minutes). Rub both sides of the tuna steaks with olive oil and season with sea salt and black pepper. Lay as many tuna steaks as you can fit in the pan and cook for about 1½–2 minutes, depending on the thickness and how rare you like them. Turn them over and cook the other side for 1–1½ minutes. Set aside on a warmed serving dish and cover lightly with foil. Repeat with the remaining steaks. Rinse the pan under hot running water, dry with paper towels and reheat until very hot. Add 2 tablespoons oil and tip in the tomatoes. Cook for 1–1½ minutes, shaking the pan till the skins start to split then turn off the heat. To serve, put a small handful of rocket/arugula on each plate, top with a few tomatoes and lay the tuna steaks alongside. Drizzle the tuna and salad with olive oil and a good squeeze of lemon juice, and sprinkle over the gremolata. Serve with some authentic French crusty baguette.

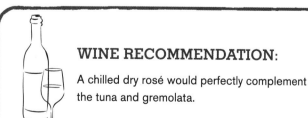

WINE RECOMMENDATION:
A chilled dry rosé would perfectly complement the tuna and gremolata.

Apricot tart with Muscat de Beaumes-de-Venise

This is a version of a brilliantly simple recipe from award-winning food writer Alastair Hendy. If you've never made a tart in your life, you could make this.

375-g/13-oz pack ready-rolled puff pastry, thawed if frozen
750 g/1½ lb. ripe apricots
2 tablespoons ground almonds
2 tablespoons caster/superfine sugar
2 tablespoons Muscat de Beaumes-de-Venise
3 tablespoons soft-set apricot jam
Greek yogurt or vanilla ice cream, to serve

a shallow, rectangular, non-stick baking pan

Serves 6

Preheat the oven to 225°C (425°F) Gas 7 and take the pastry out of the fridge about 10 minutes before you want to unroll it.

Halve and pit the apricots (you can cut the bigger ones into thirds). Unroll the pastry and lay it in the baking pan, trimming off any pastry that overhangs the edges. Prick the base with the prongs of a fork and shake over the ground almonds in an even layer. Sprinkle over 1 tablespoon of the sugar. Arrange the apricot halves or thirds in rows over the surface of the tart, leaving a narrow border around the edge and propping up each row on the one behind it. Spoon over the remaining sugar. Bake in the preheated oven for 30–35 minutes until the pastry is risen and the edges of the fruit are beginning to caramelize.

Spoon the jam into a small saucepan, add the Muscat and warm gently over low heat, stirring until smooth. Brush the warm glaze over the apricots and serve the tart with Greek yogurt or vanilla ice cream.

WINE RECOMMENDATION:
Serve extra glasses of Muscat de Beaumes-de-Venise alongside.

A Summer Picnic

Picnic food doesn't have to be rough and ready, as this sophisticated menu shows. Get ahead by making the Sun-dried Tomato, Olive and Basil Bread, Lavender Shortbread and Homemade Lemonade in advance, leaving you only the Chicken Tonnato Pasta Salad to assemble on the day (watch out – everyone is going to want the recipe!) Short of time? The menu is easy to adapt to a deli-bought meal. Just buy a nice quiche, some ready-made shortbread and some of the lovely lemonades that are now available.

Sun-dried tomato, olive
and basil bread

*

Chicken tonnato pasta salad

*

Lavender shortbread

*

Homemade lemonade

*

To Drink

Rosé is the perfect wine for this summery menu.
A drier style from southern France or Spain (where it is called rosado) would work well, but if you prefer the fuller, fruitier New World style that is more like a light red, by all means go for it. The important thing is to keep it cold. Chill well beforehand and transport in insulated bags.

Sun-dried tomato, olive and basil bread

These easy breads are very popular in France where they somewhat confusingly call them 'cake'. They're like a cross between a savoury bread and a quiche, and delicious to nibble with drinks. Being easily transportable, too, they are perfect picnic fare.

175 g/1⅓ cups plain/all-purpose flour

1 tablespoon baking powder

3 large eggs

100 ml/⅓ cup long-life milk

100 ml/⅓ cup olive oil

100 g/3½ oz. mature Gruyère cheese, grated

100 g/3½ oz. sun-dried tomatoes in oil*, drained and roughly chopped

60 g/2 oz. pitted black olives marinated with herbs, roughly chopped

a small handful of basil leaves, roughly sliced

sea salt and freshly ground black pepper

salami slices, to serve

a 21 x 11-cm/12 x 4-inch rectangular, non-stick loaf pan, lightly greased and floured

Serves 6

Preheat the oven to 180°C (350°F) Gas 4. Sift the flour with the baking powder and season well with salt and black pepper. Whisk the eggs and whisk in the milk and oil. Tip two-thirds of the liquid into the flour, beat well, then add the remaining liquid. Mix in the Gruyère, tomatoes, olives and basil, then tip into the prepared loaf pan. Bake in the preheated oven for 50 minutes or until a skewer comes out clean. Cool, then remove from the pan. Wrap in foil and keep in the fridge. Serve at room temperature, sliced and cut into halves or squares. You could also serve a plate of some chunky handcut, slices of salami that can be eaten with your fingers.

* If the sun-dried tomatoes come in oil, use a couple of tablespoons of the tomato-flavoured oil to replace the olive oil in this recipe.

Chicken tonnato pasta salad

This is a really easy yet impressive pasta salad. Don't be daunted by the rather long list of ingredients – the gremolata is based on pretty well the same ingredients as the sauce, but simply chopped rough for added texture.

500 ml/2 cups fresh chicken stock or made with 1 organic stock/bouillon cube

250 ml/1 cup dry white wine

1 small onion, sliced

1 celery stick, trimmed and cut into 3 pieces

1 bay leaf

2 slices of unwaxed lemon

8–10 black peppercorns

4 skinless, boneless chicken breasts (about 600 g/1 lb. 5 oz. in total)

200 g/7 oz. dried egg pasta shapes, such as Campanelle

8 halved, grilled artichoke hearts (optional)

1 tablespoon roughly chopped flat leaf parsley

For the dressing:

100 g/3½ oz. premium (preferably Spanish) tuna, drained of oil

2 tablespoons small capers, rinsed

about 2 tablespoons freshly squeezed lemon juice

3 canned or bottled anchovy fillets, rinsed and finely chopped

200 g/1 cup good-quality mayonnaise

a pinch of cayenne pepper

For the gremolata:

5–6 canned or jarred anchovy fillets, rinsed and chopped

2 spring onions/scallions, trimmed and thinly sliced

grated zest of 1 small unwaxed lemon or ½ large one

1 tablespoon small capers

3 tablespoons chopped flat leaf parsley

Also pack:

3 Little Gem/Boston lettuces, washed and crisped in the fridge, or a bag of mixed salad leaves or rocket/arugula

500 g/1lb. cherry tomatoes

a small bottle of olive oil

crusty bread, to serve

Serves 6

Pour the stock and wine into a saucepan big enough to take the chicken breasts in a single layer. Bring to the boil, add the onion, celery, bay leaf, lemon and peppercorns and simmer for 5 minutes. Add the chicken breasts to the stock, adding some boiling water, if needed, to cover them. Bring back to the boil, then turn the heat down and simmer very slowly for another 5 minutes. Turn off the heat, cover the pan and let the chicken cool in the stock (this will take about 4–5 hours).

To make the dressing, put the tuna in a food processor with the capers, lemon juice and anchovy fillets and whizz to a paste. Add the mayonnaise and cayenne pepper and whizz again until smooth. Turn into a large bowl. Put all the ingredients for the gremolata on a chopping board and chop them together.

Cook the pasta following the instructions on the packet and refresh with cold water.

Remove the chicken from the poaching liquid and cut into rough chunks. Add the chicken, pasta and gremolata to the dressing and toss lightly. Check the seasoning, adding more lemon juice or cayenne pepper to taste if you think it needs it (you shouldn't need salt). Transfer to a large plastic box, arrange the artichoke hearts, if using, over the top and sprinkle with parsley.

To assemble, put a handful of salad leaves on each plate, scatter over a few tomatoes, drizzle over a little olive oil, then spoon the salad on top. Serve with crusty bread.

WINE RECOMMENDATION:

A well-chilled rosé, particularly a drier style from southern France.

Homemade lemonade

You will need a juicer to make this absolutely delicious, traditional-style lemonade – in fact, it's almost worth buying one just to make it.

150 g/¾ cup caster/superfine sugar
4 large juicy unwaxed lemons, plus 1 extra, sliced, to garnish
1 litre/4 cups still or sparkling mineral water, chilled
a few sprigs of mint
plenty of ice, to serve

Makes 6–8 glasses

Put the sugar in a saucepan with 150 ml/⅔ cup water. Heat over low heat, stirring until the sugar has completely dissolved, then bring to the boil and boil for 5 minutes without stirring. Take off the heat and leave to cool. Cut 2 of the lemons into small chunks and pass through the feeder tube of a juicer. They should produce about 150 ml/⅔ cup thick juice. Squeeze the remaining lemons (again, that should yield about 150 ml/⅔ cup) and add to the other juice. Stir in the sugar syrup you've made.

Chill the lemon concentrate until ready to use. Either pour into a large jug/pitcher full of ice and pour in an equal amount of chilled still or sparkling mineral water or pour a couple of shots of lemonade into a tumbler full of ice and top up with chilled mineral water. Garnish with lemon slices and sprigs of mint.

Lavender shortbread

Homemade shortbread is unbelievably easy to make. Cornflour/cornstarch will make it smoother; ground rice or fine semolina more crumbly and rustic.

75 g/⅓ cup caster/superfine sugar, plus extra for sprinkling
175 g/1½ sticks butter, at room temperature
¼–½ teaspoon concentrated lavender essence or 1 tablespoon finely chopped dried lavender flowers
175 g/1⅓ cups plain/all-purpose flour
75 g/½ cup cornflour/cornstarch, ground rice or fine semolina

a 27 x 18-cm/11 x 7-inch, shallow, rectangular baking pan

Makes 18 shortbreads

Preheat the oven to 150°F (300°C) Gas 2. Put the sugar and butter in a food processor and process until light and fluffy (or beat together with an electric hand whisk). Add the lavender essence or flowers and whizz again. Add half the flour and pulse to incorporate, then add the remaining flour and pulse again. Add the cornflour/cornstarch and pulse again until incorporated. (Or add in stages, by hand, beating with a wooden spoon then bring the mixture together with your hands).

Tip the mixture into a baking pan and spread out until even. Mark the shortbread with a sharp knife, dividing it into 18 squares, and prick lightly with the prongs of a fork. Bake in the preheated oven for about 40–45 minutes until pale gold in colour. Sprinkle with the remaining sugar, put back in the oven and cook for another 5 minutes. Remove the pan from the oven, set aside for 10 minutes, then cut along the lines you've marked again. Remove the shortbread squares carefully with a palate knife and lay on a wire rack to finish cooling. Store in an airtight container.

A Seafood Lunch

Even if you're not by the coast, it's great to host a seafood lunch, especially for health-conscious friends who like lighter food. Fish is such a popular option these days. Wine lovers will also appreciate the chance to share a special bottle of white wine, which this simple elegant menu will show off quite perfectly. Then, having been virtuous, everyone will fall on the gorgeous creamy dessert, a lovely summer spin on the classic Italian tiramisù.

Seafood jellies with white wine and dill

*

Sicilian-spiced seabass with grilled tomatoes and baby fennel

*

Strawberry tiramisu

*

To Drink

Serve a fine, minerally unoaked white such as Chablis, Sancerre, Pouilly Fumé or a Spanish Albariño, which won't overwhelm the delicate flavours and texture of the jellies. Carry on drinking the same wine as with the first course or pick up on the Sicilian theme with a modern Sicilian white. The dessert will pair beautifully with a well-chilled glass of Moscato d'Asti or demi-sec sparkling wine.

Seafood jellies with white wine and dill

These delectable little jellies take a bit of time to assemble, but they look really fabulous.

200 ml/¾ cup light dry white wine, such as Frascati

1½ tablespoons Thai fish sauce

6 sheets of leaf gelatine (or enough to set 600 ml/2⅓ cups of liquid)

200 g/7 oz. fresh 'queen' (small) scallops, halved

200 g/7 oz. cooked shelled prawns/shrimp, thawed if frozen

freshly squeezed juice of

1 lemon and 1 lime, strained

90 g/3 oz. smoked salmon, cut into thin strips

4–5 sprigs of dill, broken into smaller sprigs

white pepper

6 glasses or glass dishes, chilled in the fridge

Serves 6

Pour the wine into a saucepan, bring to the boil and reduce by half. Pour into a measuring jug/pitcher, add the fish sauce and any liquid from the prawns/shrimp, then top up with cold water so you have 600 ml/2⅓ cups of liquid in total. Lay the gelatine in a shallow dish and sprinkle over 3 tablespoons cold water. Pour the white wine mixture back into the saucepan and bring to the boil. Turn the heat right down, add the scallops and poach for 2 minutes. Remove the scallops with a slotted spoon and let cool. Add the soaked gelatine to the poaching liquid and stir until thoroughly dissolved. Strain the mixture into a bowl, then place that bowl in a larger bowl of iced water to cool quickly.

Marinate the cooled scallops and prawns/shrimp in the lemon and lime juice with a little white pepper. Once the stock has cooled, assemble the jellies. Drain the prawns/shrimp and scallops from their marinade and place a few of each in the bottom of each glass along with pieces of smoked salmon. Add a couple of sprigs of dill then spoon over 2–3 tablespoons of stock. Place the glasses in the fridge for the jelly to set (about 45 minutes), then repeat with the next layer and the next until all the seafood and dill is used up. (Mix up the ingredients and make sure the final layer is covered with stock.) The jellies should be ready to eat within an hour or 2, but you can make them to eat the next day. Serve with fine crispbreads and unsalted butter.

WINE RECOMMENDATION:

Try a fine unoaked white such as Chablis, Sancerre or Pouilly Fumé.

Sicilian-spiced seabass with grilled tomatoes and baby fennel

A simple dish that you can cook at the tableside if you're eating outdoors.

1 rounded teaspoon fennel seeds

1 rounded teaspoon dried oregano

1 teaspoon cumin seeds

1 teaspoon sea salt crystals

1 teaspoon green or black peppercorns

¼ teaspoon crushed chillies/ hot red pepper flakes

6 small seabass, gutted and scaled*

extra virgin olive oil spray

3 unwaxed lemons

a few bay leaves

4 baby fennel bulbs

350 g/12 oz. cherry tomatoes

wedges of lemon, to serve

6 wooden skewers, soaked in water for 30 minutes

Serves 6

Heat a gas barbecue/outdoor grill or light a charcoal barbecue.

Crush the fennel seeds, oregano, cumin seeds, salt, peppercorns and chilli/red pepper flakes together thoroughly in a mortar with a pestle. Make 3 slashes in each side of the fish with a sharp knife. Spray the fish with olive oil and rub the pounded spices over the fish and into the slits. Cut 2 of the lemons in half vertically, then cut 1½ into thin slices. Cut or tear the bay leaves into halves or thirds. Place half a slice of lemon and a piece of bay leaf in each slit. Cut each fennel bulb in quarters lengthways and thread the cherry tomatoes onto the skewers. Spray the fish, fennel and tomatoes with oil and grill over medium heat until charred, turning them halfway through, removing them as they are cooked. Serve with wedges of lemon.

• If whole fish don't appeal, you could make this recipe with **tuna or swordfish steaks.**

Conventional cooking: You could cook the fish under a conventional grill/broiler or, if you would like to use tuna or swordfish steaks, in a non-stick frying pan.

WINE RECOMMENDATION:

Continue with the first course wine or try a modern Sicilian white.

Strawberry tiramisù

This decadent, impressive looking dessert is a slight adaptation of a fantastic recipe from Italian cookery writer Valentina Harris.

400 g/14 oz. fresh ripe strawberries, hulled

5 hard amaretti biscuits/cookies

2 large eggs, separated

40 g/3 tablespoons caster/superfine sugar

¼ teaspoon vanilla extract

4 tablespoons white rum

250 g/8 oz. mascarpone cheese, at room temperature

3 tablespoons whipping cream

100 ml/⅓ cup pressed apple juice

100 g/3½ oz. savoiardi (sponge finger biscuits/ ladyfinger cookies)

a medium–large, deep, glass dessert bowl

Serves 6

Weigh out 100 g/3½ oz. strawberries and chop them finely. Slice the remaining strawberries and set aside. Put the amaretti biscuits/cookies in a plastic bag, seal, then hit them with a rolling pin until they are the consistency of coarse breadcrumbs.

Beat the egg yolks in a bowl with an electric hand whisk until pale yellow and fluffy, gradually adding the sugar as you go. Add the vanilla extract and a tablespoon of the white rum. Tip the mascarpone cheese into a large bowl, beat with a wooden spoon to soften, then gradually add the egg yolk mixture and beat until smooth. In another bowl, whisk the egg whites until they just hold a soft peak. Fold the chopped strawberries into the mascarpone cheese mixture, then carefully fold in the egg whites.

Whip the whipping cream to a similar consistency then fold that in too, together with a third of the crushed amaretti biscuits. Mix the remaining rum with the apple juice. Dip some of the savoiardi in the apple-rum mixture and lay across the base of your bowl. Reserving some sliced strawberries for decoration, arrange a layer of strawberries over the savoiardi, then cover with a layer of mascarpone cream. Repeat with 1 or 2 more layers of soaked biscuits, strawberries and mascarpone cream, finishing with the mascarpone cream. Cover the bowl tightly with clingfilm/plastic wrap and chill in the fridge for at least 5 hours.

About 1 hour before you serve up, sprinkle the remaining amaretti crumbs over the top of the tiramisù, then decorate with the remaining strawberries. Return the tiramisù to the fridge until you are ready to serve it.

WINE RECOMMENDATION:

Pair this with well-chilled Moscato d'Asti or demi-sec sparkling wine.

An Around-the-World Barbecue

Give your barbecue a globetrotting theme with this menu, which roams from South America to the eastern Mediterranean.

Pork and olive empanadas
Cheese empanadas
Gazpacho shots

*

Butterflied leg of lamb with cumin, lemon and garlic
Kisir

*

Sparkling Shiraz and summer berry jellies
Sparkling nectarine and blueberry jellies

*

Exotic Sea Breeze
Watermelon and strawberry cooler

*

To Drink

Serve a Chilean Sauvignon Blanc or Spanish Rueda to start, before going on to a Merlot or Shiraz with the lamb and kisir (you don't want too full-bodied a red with spicy or chargrilled foods). Ice cold lager is also standard fare for barbecues, but a blonde ale or amber lager makes much more rewarding drinking. Alternatively, try one of the jug/pitcher drinks on page 87 – a touch of sweetness really helps with chargrilled flavours.

Pork and olive empanadas

Empanadas are like mini-pasties – in fact they're believed to have been introduced to Mexico by Cornish miners who came to work in the tin and silver mines.

3 tablespoons light olive oil
450 g/1 lb. minced/ground pork
1 onion, finely chopped
1 garlic clove, finely chopped
2 tablespoons tomato purée/concentrate
½ rounded teaspoon mixed spice
125 ml/½ cup passata
1 tablespoon cider vinegar
10 large pitted green olives marinated in garlic and herbs, finely chopped
2 tablespoons finely chopped parsley
sea salt and freshly ground black pepper
500 g/1 lb. ready-made puff pastry, thawed if frozen
1 large egg, beaten

2 large baking sheets, greased

a 9-cm/3½-inch pastry cutter

Serves 8

Heat 1 tablespoon of the olive oil in a large frying pan and brown the pork. Remove to a bowl with a slotted spoon and pour off any remaining fat and meat juices. Add the remaining 2 tablespoons oil to the pan and fry the chopped onion for about 6–7 minutes until beginning to brown. Add the chopped garlic, fry for a few seconds, then return the meat to the pan. Add the tomato purée/concentrate, stir in thoroughly and cook for a minute, then add the mixed spice, passata and vinegar. Bring to the boil and simmer for 10–15 minutes until the excess liquid has been absorbed. Stir in the chopped olives and parsley and season to taste with salt and pepper. Set aside until cool (about 1 hour).

Roll out the pastry on a floured board or work surface. Cut out rounds with the pastry cutter and place a teaspoonful of the pork filling in the centre of each one. Dampen the edges with water, fold over and press the edges together. Repeat until you have used up all the pastry and filling, re-rolling the pastry as necessary. At this point you can refrigerate or freeze the empanadas until you are ready to cook them.

To cook, preheat the oven to 225°C (425°F) Gas 7. Cut a small slit in each empanada with a sharp knife. Brush with beaten egg and place on the baking sheets. Bake in the preheated oven for 8–10 minutes until puffed up and golden (slightly longer if cooking them from frozen). Serve warm.

Cheese empanadas

1 garlic clove, roughly chopped
½ teaspoon salt
225 g/8 oz. curd or cottage cheese
¼ teaspoon sweet (dulce) pimentón or paprika
2 generous tablespoons finely chopped shallot
2 generous tablespoons finely chopped parsley
salt and freshly ground black pepper

Serves 8

Put the garlic in a mortar with the salt and pound with a pestle until you have a paste. Tip into the curd cheese along with the pimentón, shallot and parsley and mix thoroughly. Season with salt and pepper. Take teaspoonfuls of the mixture and use to fill the empañadas, as described on the left.

Gazpacho shots

This wonderfully refreshing summer soup makes a perfect start to a barbecue. You could also serve it in small bowls with its usual garnish of finely chopped tomato, onion, cucumber and red pepper and a few crispy croûtons if you prefer to eat it that way.

¼–½ mild Spanish onion (about 90 g/3 oz.), roughly chopped
1 red bell pepper, deseeded and quartered
½ cucumber, peeled, deseeded and chopped
450 g/1 lb. fresh tomatoes, skinned and chopped
400-g/14-oz. can best-quality Italian tomatoes
1 garlic clove, crushed with ½ teaspoon salt or 1 teaspoon fresh garlic paste
3 tablespoons red wine vinegar
2 tablespoons extra virgin olive oil
a few sprigs of basil
salt, freshly ground black pepper, lemon juice and hot pepper sauce, (such as Tabasco), to taste
cucumber batons and very finely diced red pepper, to garnish

Makes 16 shot glasses

Put the chopped onion in a food processor, together with three-quarters of the pepper, roughly chopped, and the cucumber and whizz until smooth. Add the fresh tomatoes, whizz again and then add the canned tomatoes, the garlic paste, vinegar and olive oil and whizz again. Transfer to a bowl, add the basil, and refrigerate for a couple of hours. Remove the basil and pass the soup through a fine nylon sieve/strainer, pressing it well to extract all

the liquid. Return to the fridge until ready to serve. Add enough iced water to make a drinkable consistency, then check the seasoning, adding salt and pepper to taste, a little vinegar or a squeeze of lemon and a dash of hot pepper sauce if you like. Serve in shot glasses with a sprinkle of tiny cubes of red pepper and a cucumber baton as a swizzle stick.

WINE RECOMMENDATION:

A zesty Chilean Sauvignon Blanc would pair well with both the gazpacho and the empanadas, as would a Spanish Rueda.

Butterflied leg of lamb with cumin, lemon and garlic

A butterflied leg of lamb - one where the bone is removed and the meat opened up to create a huge flat piece of meat - is one of the tastiest, simplest and most impressive dishes to barbecue. Order it in advance from a butcher and he'll do all the hard work for you. Serve with kisir, a mixed green salad and some flatbreads.

2 large garlic cloves, chopped
1 teaspoon coarse sea salt
1 tablespoon cumin seeds
1 teaspoon coriander seeds
1 teaspoon Herbes de Provence
½ teaspoon black peppercorns
¼ teaspoon crushed chillies/hot red pepper flakes
freshly squeezed juice of 1 lemon
3 tablespoons olive oil
1 large butterflied leg of lamb
(about 2–2.5 kg/4½–5 lb.)

a large roasting pan

Serves 8

Put the garlic, salt, cumin seeds, coriander seeds, Herbes de Provence, peppercorns and chillies/hot pepper flakes in a mortar and pound with a pestle until the garlic breaks down and you have a thick paste. Gradually work in the lemon juice and oil. Work over the meat with a small, sharp knife, cutting away any excess fat, then cut the meat into 2 or 3 manageable pieces. Put the meat in a roasting pan, rub in the marinade, cover and leave in a cool place for at least 2 hours. Heat a gas barbecue/outdoor grill to high or light a charcoal barbecue and cook for 15–20 minutes, depending on the thickness of the meat and your preference, turning it halfway through the cooking time. Remove to a warmed carving plate, cover with foil and let rest for 15 minutes before slicing thinly.

WINE RECOMMENDATION:

Serve a fruity, medium-bodied red, such as Merlot or Shiraz.

Kisir

This Turkish recipe is the perfect party salad. You can vary it depending on what you have available, substituting walnuts for hazelnuts or pistachios, for example, adding some olives or some finely snipped dried apricots or replacing the dill with fresh coriander/cilantro.

250 g/1½ cups bulghur wheat
50 g/¼ cup roasted hazelnuts, chopped
50 g/¼ cup pistachio nuts, chopped
5–6 spring onions/scallions, trimmed and thinly sliced
1/2 cucumber, peeled, deseeded and finely chopped
1 red ramiro or bell pepper, halved, deseeded and finely chopped
3 ripe tomatoes, skinned and finely chopped
1 pomegranate
freshly squeezed juice of 2 lemons
½ teaspoon salt

1 teaspoon ground cumin
1 teaspoon chilli/hot red pepper flakes
3 tablespoons extra virgin olive oil
1 tablespoon pomegranate syrup or 2 teaspoons balsamic vinegar with 1 teaspoon sugar
5 tablespoons finely chopped parsley
3 tablespoons finely chopped mint leaves
3 tablespoon finely chopped dill
sea salt and freshly ground black pepper

Serves 8

Put the bulghur wheat in a large heatproof bowl and pour over enough boiling water to just cover the grain. Leave for 15 minutes for the liquid to absorb, then pour over plenty of cold water, swirl the grain around and tip into a sieve/strainer. Squeeze the grain with your hands to extract any excess water and return the grain to the bowl.

Add the nuts, spring onions/scallions, and cucumber, pepper and tomatoes (including the seeds and pulp). Halve the pomegranate and scoop out the seeds, reserving the juice and discarding the pith. Add the pomegranate seeds to the salad.

Whisk the reserved pomegranate juice with the lemon juice, salt, cumin and chilli/hot pepper flakes, then whisk in the olive oil and pomegranate syrup and season with salt and pepper. Tip into the salad and mix well.

Finally, mix in the chopped herbs. Toss well together and check the seasoning, adding more salt, pepper or lemon juice to taste. Cover and set aside for at least an hour before serving for the flavours to infuse.

Sparkling Shiraz and summer berry jellies

9 sheets of gelatine (or enough to set 750 ml/3 cups of liquid)
1 bottle (750 ml/3 cups) sparkling Shiraz or other sparkling red wine
600 g/1 lb. 5 oz. mixed fresh red berries, such as strawberries, raspberries, blackberries, blueberries, blackcurrants or redcurrants
2–3 tablespoons sugar, depending on how ripe your berries are
6–8 tablespoons homemade sugar syrup* or shop-bought gomme
8 glasses or small glass serving dishes

Serves 8

Put the gelatine in a flat dish and sprinkle over 4 tablespoons cold water. Leave to soak for 3 minutes until soft. Heat the wine in a microwave or saucepan until hot but not boiling. Tip the gelatine into the wine and stir to dissolve, then set aside to cool. Rinse the berries, cut the strawberries into halves or quarters, then put them in a shallow bowl, sprinkle over the sugar and leave them to macerate. Check the liquid jelly for sweetness, adding sugar syrup to taste.

Put an assortment of berries in the glasses, then pour over enough jelly to cover them. Put in the fridge to chill. As soon as the jelly has set (about 1 hour) add the rest of the fruit and jelly. Return the jellies to the fridge to set for another 45 minutes–1 hour before serving.

• To make the sugar syrup, dissolve 125 g/½ cup sugar in 150 ml/½ cup water. Heat gently together in a pan. When all the grains are dissolved, bring to the boil and simmer for 2–3 minutes. Use it immediately or cool and store it for up to two weeks in the fridge.

Sparkling nectarine and blueberry jellies

9 sheets of gelatine (or enough to set 750 ml/3 cups of liquid)
750 ml/3 cups sparkling peach-flavoured wine
3 ripe nectarines
2 tablespoons freshly squeezed lemon juice
200 g/7 oz. fresh blueberries, rinsed
8 glasses or small glass serving dishes

Serves 8–10

Put the gelatine in a flat dish and sprinkle over 4 tablespoons cold water. Leave to soak for 3 minutes until soft. Heat the wine in a microwave or saucepan until hot but not boiling. Tip the gelatine into the wine and stir to dissolve, then set aside to cool. Cut the nectarines into cubes and sprinkle with the lemon juice. Put a few blueberries and cubes of nectarine in the bottom of each glass then pour over jelly to cover. Put in the fridge to chill. As soon as the jelly has set, add the remaining fruit and jelly. Return to the fridge to set for another 45 minutes–1 hour before serving.

Exotic Sea Breeze

A variation on the classic cocktail.

200 ml/7 fl oz. vodka
400 ml/14 fl oz. pomegranate juice
300 ml/10 fl oz. ruby grapefruit juice
100 ml/3½ fl oz. freshly squeezed lime juice
(from 2–3 limes)
2–3 teaspoons pomegranate syrup
1 pomegranate, halved and sliced
a few sprigs of fresh mint
ice cubes, to serve

Makes 6–8 glasses

Pour the vodka, pomegranate juice, grapefruit juice and lime
juice into a large jug/pitcher filled with ice. Sweeten to taste
with pomegranate syrup. Garnish with pomegranate seeds and
sprigs of mint to serve.

Watermelon and strawberry cooler

You can't really make this unless you have a juicer, but
otherwise it's one of the easiest and most refreshing
summer drinks.

1 large watermelon
500 g/1 lb. fresh strawberries, hulled,
plus extra to garnish
1 unwaxed lemon, peeled and chopped
100 ml/3½ fl oz. vodka (optional)
3 sprigs of mint, leaves roughly torn
ice cubes, to serve

Makes 6–8 glasses

Cut the watermelon in half, then cut off a thin slice for
garnishing. Scoop out the pulp and cut into rough chunks.
Feed the watermelon, strawberries and lemon chunks through
the juicer alternately. Put ice cubes into a jug/pitcher (plus the
vodka, if using). Pour over the juice. Add the mint and stir well.
Pour into highball glasses and decorate with a wedge of
watermelon and a few slices of strawberry to serve.

Cooling Food for a Hot Evening

It might seem a contradiction to suggest that the ideal food to serve on a sultry evening is spicy food, but if you think about those countries that habitually have hot weather like India or Thailand, you realize that that is exactly what you need. What you will also notice is that they serve it lukewarm or cold so that the heat doesn't become overwhelming. This is an eclectic modern menu to serve to adventurous friends who love new tastes and flavours.

Spiced mango, carrot and chilli soup

*

Thai-style beef with tomato and herb salad

Prawn and cucumber sesame noodles

*

Pina Colada sherbet

Exotic fruits

*

To Drink

With the soup and salads, try a dry aromatic white like an Alsace Riesling, an Austrian Grüner Veltliner or a limey Australian Verdelho. A Belgian witbier (cloudy wheat beer) would also work well.

Spiced mango, carrot and chilli soup

An unusual and stunning-looking chilled soup that is wonderfully refreshing on a warm evening. Make sure your mango is ripe or you won't get the depth of flavour you need. You might want a slightly less ripe one for the garnish.

3 tablespoons grapeseed or vegetable oil

1 onion, roughly chopped

4 carrots, thinly sliced

½ teaspoon ground turmeric

1 teaspoon grated fresh ginger or ginger paste

500 ml/2 cups vegetable stock

300 g/11 oz. (peeled, stoned weight) ripe mango, diced

freshly squeezed juice of 1–1½ limes (3–4 tablespoons)

sea salt and cayenne pepper

To serve:

low-fat plain yogurt

100 g/3½ oz. mango, peeled and cut into small dice, to serve

sweet chilli sauce

a few coriander/cilantro leaves

Japanese rice crackers, to serve (optional)

Serves 4–6

Heat the oil over low heat in a large, lidded saucepan or flameproof casserole. Add the onion, stir, cover and cook gently for 5 minutes. Add the carrots, stir, replace the lid and continue to cook for another 10 minutes. Stir in the turmeric and ginger, cook for a minute then pour in the vegetable stock. Bring to the boil and simmer until the carrot is cooked – about 20 minutes. Set aside until cool (about an hour).

Strain off the liquid into a bowl and tip the vegetables into a food processor along with the mango. Add 2–3 tablespoons of the liquid and whizz until smooth. Add half the remaining liquid and whizz again. Tip the purée into the bowl with the rest of the liquid and mix well. Add 3 tablespoons of the lime juice and season with salt and cayenne pepper. Cover and refrigerate for at least 2 hours.

To serve, pour in enough chilled water to create a thin, spoonable consistency. Check the seasoning, adding extra lime juice to taste if needed. Ladle the soup into bowls and spoon over a swirl of yoghurt. Scatter with a few cubes of mango, drizzle over a little sweet chilli sauce and scatter with coriander/cilantro leaves. Serve with Japanese rice crackers on the side.

WINE RECOMMENDATION:

A dry aromatic white wine, such as an Alsace Riesling, Austrian Grüner Veltliner or Australian Verdelho.

Thai-style beef with tomato and herb salad

Thai cuisine features some great meat-based salads that are wonderfully zingy and refreshing. The amount of chilli you use is up to you. You can leave out the roasted chillies and only use fresh ones if you like, but they do add a lovely smoky flavour to the dish.

2 tablespoons Thai fragrant rice

1 teaspoon crushed chillies

1–2 thick slices of rump steak (about 900 g/2 lb. in total and about 2½ cm/1 inch thick), trimmed of any fat

1½ tablespoons sunflower or light olive oil

3–4 teaspoons caster/superfine sugar freshly squeezed juice of 3 limes, (about 7–9 tablespoons)

4 tablespoons Thai fish sauce

2 large garlic cloves, grated

2–3 medium-hot fresh red chillies, deseeded and very finely chopped

8 small shallots, very thinly sliced or a bunch of spring onions/scallions, trimmed and thinly sliced

5 generous tablespoons coriander/cilantro leaves, chopped

3 generous tablespoons mint leaves, chopped

250 g/9 oz. cherry tomatoes, quartered

1 cos/romaine lettuce heart, washed and crisped in the fridge

a ridged stove-top grill pan

Serves 6–8

Heat a small frying pan over medium heat, add the rice and cook, stirring occasionally until golden and fragrant (about 5 minutes). Take off the heat, allow to cool for a couple of minutes, then grind in a mortar with a pestle or the end of a rolling pin. Toast the crushed chillies in the same way for a few seconds, add to the rice and grind again. Heat a ridged grill pan for about 3 minutes until smoking hot, rub the steak with the oil and cook for about 1½ minutes each side until charred but still rare (or longer if you prefer). Set aside to cool while you make the dressing.

Dissolve the sugar in the lime juice, add the fish sauce, the garlic and half the chopped chillies and taste. Add more fish sauce and chillies if you think the dressing needs it and a little water if the dressing is too strong. Slice the steak thinly, then tip the slices together with any juices into a bowl with the dressing and add the shallots, coriander/cilantro, mint and cherry tomatoes. Toss, then sprinkle with the toasted rice mixture. Finely shred the cos/romaine lettuce and arrange the shredded leaves on a large platter. Top with the dressed beef to serve.

WINE RECOMMENDATION:

A dry aromatic white wine pairs well with the gentle heat in this salad.

Prawn and cucumber sesame noodles

A clean, refreshing noodle salad that goes particularly well with the beef.

250 g/9 oz. fine rice or dried soba noodles

400 g/14 oz. cooked shelled prawns/shrimp

2/3 cucumber, peeled, quartered, deseeded and cut into diagonal slices

½ bunch of spring onions/ scallions, trimmed and thinly sliced

For the dressing:

6 tablespoons Japanese seasoned rice vinegar

2 tablespoons light soy sauce

4 tablespoons sunflower or rapeseed oil

2 tablespoons sesame oil

1½ teaspoons finely grated fresh ginger or ginger paste

1½ teaspoons finely grated garlic or garlic paste

4 tablespoons toasted sesame seeds

5 tablespoons finely chopped coriander/cilantro leaves

sea salt (optional)

Serves 6–8

Break the dried noodles into thirds and put them in a heatproof bowl. Pour over boiling water, leave for 3 minutes, then drain and rinse under cold water. Put them in a large serving bowl and add the prawns/shrimp, cucumber and spring onions/scallions.

Pour the rice vinegar and soy sauce into a separate bowl, then whisk in the sunflower and sesame oils, ginger and garlic. Add the dressing to the noodles and toss together. Check the seasoning, adding a little salt if necessary. Just before serving, sprinkle over the sesame seeds and chopped coriander/cilantro and toss again.

Piña Colada sherbet

This dessert is a cross between an ice cream and a sorbet. It makes a fantastically refreshing end to the meal. Don't make it more than a few days in advance, as it won't keep like a commercial ice cream.

150 g/¾ cup caster/superfine sugar

1 ripe pineapple

200 ml/¾ cup coconut cream

6 tablespoons freshly squeezed

lime juice (2–3 limes)

4 tablespoons white rum

2 large egg whites, beaten

Serves 6–8

Put the sugar in a pan with 200 ml/¾ cup water over very low heat, stirring occasionally, until the sugar has dissolved. Bring to the boil without stirring and boil for about 4 minutes. Set aside to cool. Quarter the pineapple, cut away the tough central core and cut off the skin. Cut into cubes and pass through a juicer.* This should give you about 550–600 ml/2½ cups juice. Mix in the coconut cream, cooled sugar syrup, lime juice and rum, which should give you just over 1 litre/4 cups liquid.

Cover, transfer the sherbet mixture to the fridge and chill for a couple of hours. Pour into an ice cream machine and churn, adding the egg whites halfway through. (You may need to do this in 2 batches). If you haven't got an ice cream machine, pour the sherbet mix into a lidded plastic box and freeze for about 1½ hours or until beginning to harden at the edges. Put the egg whites in a food processor, process briefly until frothy, then tip in the half-frozen sherbet mixture and whizz until smooth. Return the sherbet mix to the freezer, freeze for another hour, then whizz again. Freeze and whizz a third time for extra smoothness. Leave to harden. Before serving, remove the sherbet from the freezer and leave to mellow in the fridge for about 20 minutes. Serve with a selection of tropical fruits.

• If you haven't got a juicer, remove all the little brown 'eyes' from the pineapple, cut into cubes, purée in a food processor and strain the juice.

Exotic fruits

Make up a large, attractive platter of exotic fruits such as pineapple, mango, papaya, passion fruit, star fruit, physalis and lychees so that your guests can help themselves.

Winter Menus

A Midwinter Supper

Fennel, leek and cauliflower soup • Pot roast brisket with Zinfandel
Cavolo nero • Roast pumpkin and garlic polenta
Orange and Cointreau syllabub

A French Bistro Supper

Gougères • Beaujolais Kir • Charcuterie and radishes • Boeuf bourguignon
Pomme purée • Sheeps' cheese with cherry compôte • Chocolate pots with Maury

A Moroccan-Inspired Supper

Grilled pepper, tomato and chilli salad • Spiced carrot and black olive salad
Moroccan ratatouille • Green couscous • Chicken, lemon and green olive tagine
Orange flower water salad • Moroccan mint tea

A Vegetarian Harvest Supper

Pumpkin soup with honey and sage • Heirloom tomato, pepper and mozzarella tart
Steamed new potatoes with butter, parsley and chives • Garden salad •
Caramelized figs with cinnamon and sweet sherry • Brandy snaps

A Family Sunday Lunch

Homemade cheese nibbles • Parmesan and pistachio biscuits • Cheddar crispies
Superlative roast chicken with sausage meatballs • Crunchy roast potatoes
Buttery peas • Raspberry, apple and almond crumble

A Midwinter Supper

When it's cold outside, nothing is nicer than to sit around a candlelit table and enjoy a good meal served with the perfect wine. This menu is full of warm, comforting flavours – a smooth vegetable soup, an old-fashioned pot roast served with gorgeous rich polenta and an indulgent, creamy dessert that's guaranteed to make you feel that the winter isn't so bad after all.

Fennel, leek and cauliflower soup

*

Pot roast brisket with Zinfandel
Cavolo nero
Roast pumpkin and garlic polenta

*

Orange and Cointreau syllabub

*

To Drink

Soup isn't the easiest dish to pair with wine (two liquids together don't always work) but the creamy texture of this fennel soup goes well with a crisp, dry, fresh white such as a Chablis or other unoaked white Burgundy. With the pot roast brisket you want a robust, warming red – a good Zinfandel or a Cabernet Sauvignon would be my top recommendations. The syllabub would work well with a small glass of Australian botrytized Semillon.

Fennel, leek and cauliflower soup

This deceptively creamy soup doesn't actually contain cream. Try if you can to use organic vegetables to make it: you really will be able to taste the difference.

2 tablespoons olive oil

25 g/2 tablespoons unsalted butter

2 leeks, trimmed and sliced

1 large or 2 small bulbs of fennel, trimmed and sliced (reserve the feathery leaves if they're still on the bulb)

1 large garlic clove, crushed

1 small or ½ large cauliflower

1 litre/4 cups fresh chicken or vegetable stock

1 bay leaf

2–3 sprigs fresh tarragon or 1 teaspoon dried tarragon

2–3 tablespoons whole milk (optional)

a small pinch of mace

sea salt and freshly ground white or black pepper

a few fennel, dill or parsley leaves and some chives, to garnish

Serves 6

Heat the oil for a minute in a large saucepan, then add the butter. When the foaming dies down, add the leeks, fennel and garlic, stir, cover and cook over a low heat for 8–10 minutes. Meanwhile, remove the florets from the cauliflower. Add them to the pan, stir and cook for another 3–4 minutes. Pour the stock over the vegetables, add the bay leaf and tarragon and bring to the boil. Partially cover the pan and simmer for 15 minutes or until the cauliflower and fennel are soft. Remove from the heat and allow to cool slightly. Remove the bay leaf and tarragon. Strain the soup, reserving the liquid.

Put the vegetables in food processor and whizz until smooth, adding as much of the reserved liquid as you need to make a smooth, creamy consistency. Whizz the remaining liquid in the blender or food processor to pick up the last scraps of vegetable purée and add to the soup in the pan. Reheat gently, diluting the soup with a little more stock or milk if it seems too thick. Season to taste with salt, pepper and mace.

Chop the reserved fennel leaves or some dill or parsley and cut the chives into approximately 1½-cm/ ⅔-inch lengths. Serve the soup in individual bowls, scatter with the herbs and serve with some light rye or multigrain bread.

WINE RECOMMENDATION:

A crisp, dry fresh white from France such as a Chablis or other unoaked white Burgundy.

Pot roast brisket with Zinfandel

Brisket is a much underrated cut with a rich flavour that lends itself well to braising. You can use any full-bodied red, but Zinfandel has just the right gutsy rustic character.

250 ml/1 cup Zinfandel or full-bodied red wine

250 ml/1 cup fresh beef stock

2 tablespoons red wine vinegar

1 large garlic clove, crushed

1 bay leaf

1 onion, chopped

a few of sprigs of thyme or ½ teaspoon dried thyme

1.5 kg/3½ lb. boned, rolled brisket of beef

2–3 tablespoons light olive oil

2 tablespoons dry Marsala or Madeira

sea salt and freshly ground pepper

a *flameproof casserole*

Serves 6

Mix the wine and stock with the wine vinegar, garlic, bay leaf, onion and thyme. Put the meat in a sturdy plastic bag, pour over the marinade and pull the top of the bag together tightly so that the liquid covers the meat. Knot the top of the bag or seal with a wire tie. Leave the meat to marinate in the fridge for at least 4 hours or overnight.

Preheat the oven to 200°C (400°F) Gas 6. Remove the meat from the marinade and dry thoroughly with paper towels. Strain the marinade and reserve the liquid. Heat the oil in a flameproof casserole. Brown the meat all over in the hot oil then add 3–4 tablespoons of the strained marinade. Put a lid on the casserole and roast for 2 hours. Check from time to time that the pan juices are not burning. Add more marinade if necessary, but the flavour of this dish comes from the well-browned sticky juices, so do not add too much extra liquid. If on the other hand more liquid has formed, spoon some out. Simmer the remaining marinade over low heat until it loses its raw, winey taste.

Once the meat is cooked, set it aside in a warm place. Spoon any fat off the surface of the pan juices and add the Marsala and the cooked marinade. Bring to the boil, scraping off all the brown tasty bits from the side of the casserole and adding a little extra water if necessary. Season to taste with salt and pepper and serve spooned over slices of the meat or in a gravy boat for pouring.

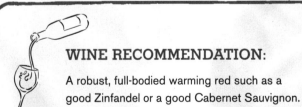

WINE RECOMMENDATION:

A robust, full-bodied warming red such as a good Zinfandel or a good Cabernet Sauvignon.

Cavolo nero

3 heads of cavolo nero or spring greens
3 tablespoons olive oil
1 garlic clove, thinly sliced
sea salt and freshly ground black pepper

Serves 6

Pull the leaves off the stalks and tear out the central tough rib of each leaf. Slice the greens and put in a saucepan. Pour over just enough boiling water to cover, bring back to the boil and cook for 2–3 minutes. Drain the greens. Add the oil to the saucepan and cook the garlic very gently without colouring until soft and sweet (about 5 minutes). Toss the greens in the garlic-flavoured oil and cook over low heat for 5 minutes. Season to taste and serve.

Roast pumpkin and garlic polenta

Polenta normally has lavish amounts of butter and cheese added to give it flavour, but here's a much lighter version made with roast pumpkin and roast garlic, which you can cook at the same time as the beef (see page 95).

1 medium pumpkin or 1 large butternut squash
5 large garlic cloves, unpeeled
3 tablespoons sunflower or grapeseed oil
40 g/3 tablespoons butter
50 g/½ cup grated Parmesan cheese, plus extra to taste
1.2 litres/5 cups vegetable stock, plus a little extra as necessary
250 g/1²/₃ cups good-quality Italian polenta
sea salt and freshly ground black pepper

a large roasting pan

Serves 6

Preheat the oven to 190°C (375°F) Gas 5. Halve the pumpkin. Cut one half into quarters and scoop out the seeds. Quarter the other half, scoop out the seeds, cut each quarter into 2 or 3 pieces and cut away the skin with a sharp knife. Put all the pumpkin in a roasting pan along with the garlic cloves. Drizzle with the oil, mix well together and season generously with salt and pepper. Roast in the preheated oven for about 35–40 minutes until soft.

Remove the quartered pumpkin from the pan and set the rest aside to be reheated just before serving. Scrape the flesh off the skin and put in a food processor. Pop the roasted garlic cloves out of their skins and add to the pumpkin and whizz until smooth. Add the butter and Parmesan, whizz again and season with salt and pepper. Cook the polenta in the vegetable stock, following the instructions on the packet, taking care to whisk well to avoid lumps. Add the pumpkin and garlic purée to the cooked polenta and mix well. Add a little extra stock if needed to give a slightly sloppy consistency. Check the seasoning, adding more salt, pepper and Parmesan to taste. Reheat the pumpkin pieces briefly in a microwave or frying pan. Serve topped with pumpkin pieces.

Orange and Cointreau syllabub

Syllabub – a delicious, velvety smooth concoction of sweet wine and cream – is one of the great English desserts, dating from the 16th century. Top with a sprinkling of orange zest and sugar.

150 ml/²/₃ cup southern French Muscat or other strong sweet white wine (minimum 15% ABV)

1 tablespoon Cointreau or other orange-flavoured liqueur

finely grated zest of 2 unwaxed oranges

2 tablespoons freshly squeezed orange juice

2 tablespoons freshly squeezed lemon juice

4 tablespoons caster/superfine sugar

400 ml/1¾ cups double/heavy cream, chilled

a large bowl, chilled for 30–40 minutes in the fridge or for 15–20 minutes in the freezer

6 small glass tumblers or dishes

Serves 6

Pour the wine into a bowl, add the Cointreau, half the grated orange zest, the orange and lemon juice and 2 tablespoons of the sugar. Stir, cover and refrigerate for several hours or overnight. Pass through a fine sieve/strainer. Pour the cream into the chilled bowl and beat with an electric hand whisk until it starts to thicken. Gradually add the chilled wine mixture, beating between each addition until the cream thickens again. (Don't overbeat it, or it will separate.) Aim for a thick pouring consistency. When the final addition of wine has been incorporated, the mixture should hold a trail when you lift out the beaters, but shouldn't be stiff.) Ladle the mixture into tumblers and chill for at least an hour before serving. In the meantime, mix the remaining orange zest and sugar, and leave it on a plate to crisp up. Just before serving, sprinkle the orange sugar over the top of each glass.

WINE RECOMMENDATION:

If you want to serve wine with this dish, try a botrytized Semillon.

A French Bistro Supper

A perfect menu for entertaining, as pretty well everything can be cooked in advance or assembled on the day. You don't necessarily need all the courses – the charcuterie would make a meal in itself, for instance, and you could skip the cheese – but it does make a wonderfully lavish spread. Given the all-French menu, it seems almost sacrilege to drink anything but French wine, although you could give it an unusual twist by serving red throughout.

Gougères
Beaujolais Kir
Charcuterie and radishes

*

Boeuf bourguignon
Pomme purée

*

Sheeps' cheese with cherry compôte

*

Chocolate pots with Maury

*

To Drink

Kick off with a Beaujolais Kir with the gougères and then a Beaujolais with the charcuterie and radishes. Accompany the beef and the sheeps' cheese with a robust Rhône or Languedoc red. The chocolate pots with Maury are prefect served with a glass of the same sweet, red dessert wine.

Gougères

A classic French 'nibble' – just perfect with
a Beaujolais Kir (see right).

50 g/3 tablespoons butter, cut into cubes
75 g/½ cup strong white/all-purpose flour, sifted with
¼ teaspoon salt and a pinch of cayenne pepper
1 medium and 2 large eggs
50 g/½ cup finely grated well-matured Gruyère cheese,
2 baking sheets, lightly greased

Makes 20–24

Preheat the oven to 220°C (425°F) Gas 7. Measure
150 ml/²/₃ cup water into a saucepan and add the butter.
Heat gently until the butter has melted, then bring to the boil.
Remove from the heat and add the sifted flour mixture. Beat
vigorously until the mixture forms a ball and leaves the side of
the pan clean. Set aside for 5 minutes. Beat 2 eggs and
gradually add them to the pastry, working them in until the
mixture is smooth and glossy. Add all except 1 generous
tablespoon of the cheese. Run the baking sheets under the
tap and then shake off any excess water. Place teaspoonfuls
of the mixture onto each sheet. Beat the remaining egg and
brush the top of each puff lightly with a pastry brush. Sprinkle
with the remaining cheese. Bake in the preheated oven for
about 25 minutes until puffed up and golden. Remove the
gougères from the oven and cut a small slit in the base of
each to let the hot air escape. Cool on a wire rack.

Beaujolais Kir

1 small (50-cl) bottle crème de cassis (blackcurrant-flavoured
liqueur), chilled
2 x bottles (75-cl) of Beaujolais Villages, chilled

Makes 12 glasses

Pour a good splash of crème de cassis into each glass and top
up with the Beaujolais. Aim for about 1 part crème de cassis to
4 parts wine.

Charcuterie and radishes

One of the easiest possible starters – which is why so
many French bistros serve it. If you want to do it French-
style, buy some slices of air-dried ham, some whole
saucisson and a thick slice of pâté or rillettes (which
you can transfer to a small pottery bowl and pretend is
your own!) Wash a couple of bunches of fresh radishes,
cutting the leaves off a few centimetres above the base
of the stem. Lay on some good French artisanal butter
(the kind with salt crystals is perfect with this), some
crusty baguette and a sharp Laguiole knife to cut the
sausage. Almost a meal in itself!

WINE RECOMMENDATION:
Serve a Beaujolais Kir with the gougères,
moving on to a Beaujolais with the charcuterie
and radishes.

Boeuf bourguignon

Although Boeuf Bourguignon sounds as if it should be made from red Burgundy, a fuller-bodied red from the Rhône or Languedoc works very well. You can make it a day ahead to allow the flavours to develop, but it's not essential to do so.

900 g/2 lb. braising beef/beef chuck or steak
3 tablespoons olive oil
130 g/4½ oz. cubed pancetta
3 onions, finely chopped
2 large garlic cloves, finely chopped
1½ tablespoons plain/all-purpose flour
450 ml/2 cups red wine, plus an extra splash if needed
a bouquet garni made from a few sprigs of thyme, parsley stalks and a bay leaf
25 g/2 tablespoons butter
250 g/9 oz. chestnut/cremini mushrooms, cleaned and halved
2 tablespoons finely chopped flat leaf parsley
salt and freshly ground black pepper

a large, flameproof casserole

Serves 6

Pat the meat dry, trim off any excess fat or sinew and cut into large chunks. Heat 1 tablespoon of the oil in a large saucepan and fry the pancetta until lightly browned. Remove from the pan with a slotted spoon and transfer to a flameproof casserole. Brown the meat in 2 batches in the fat that remains in the pan and add to the bacon. Add the remaining oil and fry the onion slowly, covering the pan, until soft and caramelized (about 25 minutes), adding the chopped garlic halfway through the cooking time. Stir the flour into the onions, cook for a minute, then add the wine and bring to the boil. Pour over the meat, add the bouquet garni and bring back to the boil. Turn down the heat and simmer over very low heat for 2–2½ hours, until the meat is just tender. Turn off the heat and leave the casserole overnight.

The next day bring the casserole back to boiling point, then turn down low again. Heat the butter in a frying pan and fry the mushrooms until lightly browned (about 5 minutes). Tip the mushrooms into the stew, stir and cook for another 10–15 minutes. Season the casserole to taste with salt and pepper, adding an extra splash of wine if you don't think the flavour is quite pronounced enough. Sprinkle over chopped parsley before serving with pomme purée (see right) or boiled new potatoes.

Pomme purée

This is the decadent French way of cooking creamy mashed potatoes.

1 kg/2¼ lbs. red-skinned potatoes, such as Desirée or Wilja
50 ml/3 tablespoons double/heavy cream
75–100 ml/¼–⅓ cup whole milk
75 g/5 tablespoons unsalted butter, cut into cubes and at room temperature
sea salt and freshly ground black pepper

a potato ricer

Serves 6

Peel the potatoes and cut them into quarters or eighths (about half the size you would cut them for normal mash). Put them in a saucepan, pour over boiling water, add 1 teaspoon salt and bring back to the boil. Turn down the heat and simmer gently for about 12–15 minutes until you can easily pierce them with a skewer. Drain them in a colander, then return them to the pan over very low heat and leave them for a minute or 2 to dry off.

Mix the cream and milk together and heat until just below boiling point in a microwave or separate saucepan. Tip the potatoes back into the colander, then pass them through a potato ricer back into the pan. Pour in half the cream mixture and beat with a wooden spoon, then gradually beat in the remaining cream mixture and the butter. Season to taste with salt and pepper.

WINE RECOMMENDATION:

A robust Rhône or Languedoc red pairs well with both the beef and the sheeps' cheese with cherry compôte (overleaf).

Sheeps' cheese with cherry compôte

Rather than a full cheeseboard, you could serve slices of sheeps' cheese as they do in the south-west of France with a good-quality bought cherry compôte, a combination that works much better with red wine than cheese alone. Serve with thin slices of sourdough or wholemeal bread.

Chocolate pots with Maury

It's so easy to buy great chocolate desserts these days that if you're going to make them yourself you need to give them a bit of a twist. The French red dessert wine Maury, is a wonderful accompaniment for chocolate. It's very rich but chocoholics will probably want two!

200 g/7 oz. premium dark/bittersweet chocolate (minimum 70% cocoa solids)
150 ml/a generous ½ cup Maury or 100 ml/ ⅓ cup late-bottled vintage port
300 ml/1¼ cups whipping cream
2 very fresh large organic egg yolks* (optional)
1–2 tablespoons caster/superfine sugar
sifted cocoa powder and icing/confectioners' sugar, to decorate

8–10 small ramekins or espresso cups

Serves 8–10

Break the chocolate into squares, put them in a food processor and briefly blitz them to break them into small pieces. Leave them in the processor.

Heat the Maury until almost boiling and pour it over the chocolate. Heat the cream, until almost boiling, and pour that over too. Leave for a few seconds to melt the chocolate, then whizz until the chocolate is smooth. Add the egg yolks, if using, and whizz again. Check for sweetness, adding caster/superfine sugar to taste. Pour the mixture into the serving dishes and chill in the fridge for a couple of hours, removing the desserts 20 minutes before serving. Using a small tea strainer, sift a thin layer of cocoa powder over the top of each pot, then follow with a sprinkling of icing/confectioners' sugar.

* The raw egg yolks improve the texture, but you could leave them out if you prefer.

WINE WITH CHOCOLATE

Chocolate isn't the easiest ingredient to match with wine, but a sweet red like Maury is generally much more successful than a sweet white. Other reds you could consider include Mavrodaphne of Patras from Greece, Banyuls, which like Maury is from the South of France, Recioto from Italy or late-bottled vintage port, especially if there are some dark berry fruits like cherries in the dessert.

A Moroccan-inspired Feast

The subtle spicy flavours of these dishes are perfectly warming on a cold day and Moroccan food captures an exquisite balance between vegetables, meat, fruit and grain. The recipes are more time consuming to prepare than many in this book, but this is a pleasurable meal to make with family or friends who share a passion for cooking.

Grilled pepper, tomato and
chilli salad

Spiced carrot and black olive salad

Moroccan ratatouille

*

Green couscous

*

Chicken, lemon and green
olive tagine

*

Orange flower water salad

*

Moroccan mint tea and pastries

*

To Drink

Wine-wise go for a light dry rosé, such as a southern French Syrah rosé, a Spanish rosado or a mature oak-aged Spanish red like a Rioja Reserva. Although, as most Moroccans don't drink alcohol, a fruit juice, such as pomegranate, would also be a good accompaniment.

Grilled pepper, tomato and chilli salad

2 green peppers, skinned

3–4 Marmara or other long sweet peppers, skinned

400 g/14 oz. ripe tomatoes, skinned and sliced

¼ teaspoon smoked sweet (dulce) pimentón or paprika

¼ teaspoon ground cumin

1 tablespoon freshly squeezed lemon juice

2 tablespoons olive oil

2 tablespoons pickled sliced Jalapeño chillies, rinsed and finely chopped

1 generous tablespoon finely chopped parsley

sea salt and freshly ground black pepper

Serves 6

Deseed the skinned peppers, slice them thickly and put in a serving bowl with the skinned tomatoes. Measure the pimentón and cumin into another small bowl and whisk in the lemon juice and oil. Season to taste with salt and pepper. Pour the dressing over the peppers and tomatoes, add the Jalapeños and parsley and toss together.

Spiced carrot and black olive salad

350 g/12 oz. young carrots

2 tablespoons olive oil

½ teaspoon Moroccan spice mix*

a pinch each of sea salt and sugar

75 g/2½ oz. pitted black olives marinated with herbs

freshly squeezed juice of ½ orange (about 2 tablespoons)

a good squeeze of lemon juice

½ teaspoon lightly crushed roasted cumin seeds (optional)

2 tablespoons chopped coriander/cilantro

Serves 6

Cut the carrots into thin diagonal slices. Heat the oil in a saucepan over low heat, add the spice mix, and cook for a few seconds. Tip in the carrots, turn them in the spiced oil and cook gently for 3–4 minutes. Stir in the salt and sugar, add 2 tablespoons water and put a lid on the pan. Cook the carrots over low heat until they are soft (about 20 minutes), stirring occasionally and adding a little more water if the carrots start to burn.

Tip the carrots into a dish, let cool, then mix in the olives and orange juice. Season to taste with salt and lemon juice. Just before serving, sprinkle over the cumin seeds, if using, and chopped coriander/cilantro.

* To make Moroccan spice mix, combine 2 tablespoons each of ground cumin and ground coriander, 2 teaspoons turmeric and 1–1½ teaspoons chilli powder or hot (piquante) pimentón.

Moroccan rataouille

2 medium aubergines/eggplant or 1 large (about 500 g/1 lb.)

4 tablespoons olive oil

1 onion, roughly chopped

1 garlic clove, crushed

2 tomatoes, skinned, deseeded and diced

2 tablespoons chopped parsley

1 tablespoon chopped mint leaves

1–1½ tablespoons freshly squeezed lemon juice

1 teaspoon ground cumin

sea salt and freshly ground black pepper

a lidded wok

Serves 6

Slice off and discard the aubergine/eggplant stalks and cut each one in half lengthways and then into cubes. Heat a wok for about 2 minutes over high heat, add the oil and heat for a few seconds, then tip in the aubergine/eggplant cubes.

Stir-fry over medium heat for about 5 minutes until lightly browned, then turn the heat down slightly, add the onion and cook for another few minutes. Turn the heat down very low, stir in the garlic, cover the wok and cook gently for a further 10–12 minutes, stirring occasionally.

Tip the aubergine/eggplant into a shallow dish and leave to cool for about 20 minutes. Mix in the tomato, parsley and mint. Season with the lemon juice and cumin and salt and pepper to taste.

Green couscous

250 g/9 oz. courgettes/zucchini

250 ml/1 cup hot vegetable stock

250 g/9 oz. couscous

2 tablespoon olive oil

1 tablespoon finely chopped mint leaves

sea salt and freshly ground black pepper

Serves 6

Trim the ends off the courgettes/zucchini and grate them coarsely. Pour the hot stock into a heatproof bowl and sprinkle over the couscous. Leave the grains until they have absorbed the liquid then fluff them up using a fork.

Heat the oil in a large frying pan, tip in the grated courgettes/zucchini and stir-fry for 1½ minutes until still bright green but beginning to soften. Tip in the chopped mint, then tip the courgettes/zucchini into the couscous and fork through. Season to taste with salt and black pepper.

Chicken, lemon and green olive tagine

A fabulously fragrant chicken casserole that can be easily made ahead of time and reheated just before serving.

12 skinless, boneless chicken thighs (about 1 kg/2¼ lb. in total)
3 tablespoons olive oil
400 g/14 oz. onions, sliced
2 garlic cloves, crushed
a good pinch of saffron threads
300 ml/1¼ cups chicken or vegetable stock
1 teaspoon finely grated fresh ginger or ½ teaspoon ground ginger
2 small preserved lemons
75 g/2½ oz. pitted green olives marinated with herbs

a small bunch of fresh coriander/cilantro with its stalks, washed
1–2 tablespoons freshly squeezed lemon juice
sea salt and freshly ground black pepper
1 teaspoon harissa (Moroccan chilli paste), to serve

a large cast-iron casserole or lidded frying pan

Serves 6

Remove any excess fat from the chicken thighs and cut them in half. Heat the oil in the casserole or frying pan, add the sliced onions and garlic and cook over medium heat for 7–8 minutes until the onions have started to soften and collapse. Add the chicken thighs, mix well with the onions and continue to cook for about 10 minutes over low heat, stirring occasionally. Put the saffron in a mortar or small bowl and crush with a pestle. Pour over 2 tablespoons of the stock and leave for a few minutes to infuse. Stir the saffron and ginger into the chicken. Quarter the preserved lemons, scoop out the flesh and finely slice the peel. Halve the olives, then add them to the chicken along with the preserved lemon. Pour in the remaining stock and mix well. Cut the stalks off the coriander/cilantro and tie them together with a piece of cotton or string and lay them in the casserole. Put a lid on the pan and leave to simmer until the chicken is cooked (about another 30 minutes). Remove the coriander/cilantro stalks and season the tagine to taste with lemon juice, salt and pepper. Put the harissa paste into a bowl, spoon off 4–5 tablespoons of the liquid from the tagine and mix with the harissa. Roughly chop the coriander/cilantro leaves, stir into the tagine and serve the harissa on the side.

WINE RECOMMENDATION:

A light dry rosé, such as a southern French Syrah, a Spanish rosado or an oak-aged Spanish red like Rioja Reserva.

Orange flower water salad

Moroccans often serve oranges as a starter salad, but they work particularly well as the refreshing end to a meal, too.

100 g/½ cup caster/superfine sugar
6 oranges
1–2 teaspoons orange flower water, to taste
freshly squeezed lemon juice, to taste
2 tablespoons chopped pistachios (optional)

Serves 6

Put the sugar in a saucepan with 200 ml/¾ cup water and place over low heat, stirring occasionally until all the sugar crystals have dissolved and the liquid is completely clear. Bring up to the boil and boil without stirring for 3–4 minutes, then turn off the heat and leave to cool.

Using a sharp knife, score through the skin of each of the oranges, dividing them into quarters without cutting through the oranges themselves. Put in a large heatproof bowl, and pour over a kettleful of boiling water. Leave for a minute, then drain the water away and cover the oranges with cold water. Peel the oranges, removing as much of the white pith as possible. Slice the oranges across into thin slices, discarding any pips but carefully preserving the juice, then lay the orange slices in a bowl.

Mix the cooled syrup with the reserved orange juice and 1 teaspoon orange flower water and taste, adding a few more drops orange flower water if you think it needs it or a squeeze of lemon juice if too sweet. Pour over the oranges, cover and chill for a couple of hours. Sprinkle with chopped pistachios. Serve with a selection of Moroccan or Middle Eastern pastries.

Moroccan mint tea

The ingredient that makes all the difference is the green tea which counteracts the overall sweetness of the tea.

2 small handfuls of mint leaves
2 green tea bags or 3 teaspoonfuls of loose green tea
2 teaspoons caster/granulated sugar

Makes 1 large pot or 6 cups

Put the mint leaves in a teapot along with the green tea and sugar. Pour over boiling water, stir and infuse for 4–5 minutes.

Serve the tea with a selection of shop-bought Moroccan or Middle-Eastern pastries.

A Vegetarian Harvest Supper

This is a simple supper combining the best of autumn's produce with a couple of convenience products. Ready-rolled pastry has made it easy to knock up a quick, impressive tart, while a simple dessert of baked or grilled fruit dresses up a bought tub of ice cream. The soup can even be made ahead and frozen.

Pumpkin soup with honey and sage

*

Heirloom tomato, pepper and mozzarella tart

Steamed new potatoes with butter, parsley and chives

Garden salad

*

Brandy snaps

Caramelized figs with cinnamon and sweet sherry

*

To Drink

The case can be made here for artisanal cider or perry, which is cider made with pears. Pick a medium dry rather than a very dry variety, which should take you right through the first two courses of this menu. If you prefer to serve wine, pair a lightly oaked Chardonnay with the soup and a soft fruity red, like Merlot, with the tart. As the figs already include a full-bodied sweet sherry, serving a dessert wine with these is not recommended.

Pumpkin soup with honey and sage

This delicious and warming autumnal soup is based on vegetarian stock, but you could make it using chicken stock too.

75 g/5 tablespoons unsalted butter
1 small–medium onion, roughly chopped
1 carrot, finely chopped
1 garlic clove, crushed
1 kg/2¼ lb. pumpkin or butternut squash, deseeded, peeled and cut into cubes
2 generous tablespoons clear honey
3 sprigs of sage, plus extra crisp-fried leaves (optional), to serve
750 ml/3 cups vegetable stock
75 ml/⅓ cup double/heavy cream
freshly squeezed lemon juice, to taste
sea salt and freshly ground black pepper

Serves 4–6

Gently melt the butter in a large lidded saucepan or flameproof casserole. Add the onion, carrot and garlic, stir, cover and cook over low heat for about 4–5 minutes. Add the cubed pumpkin, honey and sage, stir, replace the lid and continue to cook very gently for about 10 minutes. Pour in the stock, bring to the boil and cook for a further 10 minutes until the vegetables are soft. Turn off the heat and allow the soup to cool slightly, then remove the sage and strain the soup, retaining the liquid. Put half the cooked vegetables in a food processor with just enough of the reserved cooking liquid to blend into a smooth purée. Transfer to a clean saucepan and repeat with the remaining vegetables, adding the purée to the first batch in the saucepan. Whizz the remaining liquid in the food processor to pick up the last bits of purée and add that too. Bring the soup slowly to the boil, then stir in the cream without boiling further. Season to taste with lemon juice (about 1 tablespoon), salt (about a teaspoon) and pepper.

Serve with an extra swirl of cream or scatter some crisp-fried sage leaves on top and serve with wholemeal or multigrain bread.

WINE RECOMMENDATION:

Artisanal, medium-dry cider or perry would be a good match for this soup. Or perhaps a lightly oaked Chardonnay.

Heirloom tomato, pepper and mozzarella tart

There are so many beautifully coloured tomatoes and peppers, it's easy to make this spectacular-looking tart.

375-g/13-oz. sheet of ready-rolled puff pastry, thawed if frozen

1 large or 2 small red bell peppers

1 large or 2 small yellow bell peppers

3 tablespoons olive oil

2 garlic cloves, unpeeled and flattened

4 generous tablespoons red pesto, homemade or from a jar

150 g/5½ oz. buffalo mozzarella, drained and thinly sliced

125 g/4½ oz. red cherry tomatoes, destalked and halved

125 g/4½ oz. yellow cherry tomatoes, destalked and halved

½ teaspoon dried oregano or marjoram

1 egg, lightly beaten

3 tablespoons shaved Parmesan cheese

a few basil leaves, roughly torn

sea salt and freshly ground black pepper

a rectangular baking sheet, lightly greased

Serves 4–6

Preheat the oven to 200°C (400°F) Gas 6. Take the pastry out of the fridge 20 minutes before you need it. Quarter the peppers, remove the pith and seeds and cut each quarter into half lengthways. Put in a roasting pan with the garlic cloves, pour over 2 tablespoons of oil and mix well. Roast for 20–25 minutes. Let cool for 10 minutes.

Unroll the pastry and lay on the baking sheet. Using a sharp knife, score a line around the pastry about 1¼ cm/½ inch from the edge. Spread the pesto inside the rectangle you've marked. Lay the pepper strips across the base of the tart, alternating red and yellow. Arrange the mozzarella pieces over the peppers. Season with black pepper. Lay the tomatoes over the peppers, red on yellow and yellow on red. Sprinkle the oregano over the tart, season with a little salt and a little more pepper and trickle over the remaining oil.

Turn the oven up to 220°C (425°F) Gas 7. Brush the edges of the tart with the egg and bake for about 12 minutes. Turn the heat back down again to 200°C (400°F) Gas 6 and cook for another 12–15 minutes until the tops of the tomatoes are well browned. Sprinkle a little Parmesan over the tart, then leave to cool for 5 minutes. Scatter the basil leaves over the tart to finish. Serve warm.

WINE RECOMMENDATION:
Continue with the cider or perry, or try a soft, fruity red, such as Merlot.

Steamed potatoes with butter, parsley and chives

Freshly dug potatoes have a wonderful earthy, nutty taste that's best shown off by steaming, as here.

1 kg/2¼ lb. new or waxy salad potatoes, such as Charlotte

40 g/3 tablespoons butter, melted

2 generous tablespoons chopped parsley

2 tablespoons finely snipped chives

sea salt and freshly ground black pepper

Serves 6

Scrub the potatoes, leaving the skins on, and cut into small, even-sized pieces. Steam until tender (about 7–8 minutes).

Put the potatoes in a serving dish, pour over the butter and sprinkle with the herbs. Season lightly with salt and black pepper and toss everything together. Serve warm.

Garden salad

One of the nicest things to have with a meal based on seasonal produce is a large, freshly picked salad of dark leafy greens, either from the garden or from your local farmers' market.

2 tablespoons seasoned rice vinegar

4 tablespoons sunflower oil

a pinch of sugar (optional)

200 g/7 oz. mixed dark leafy greens, such as rocket/arugula, spinach, chard and watercress

a few basil leaves (optional)

salt and freshly ground black pepper

Serves 6

Whisk together the rice vinegar and sunflower oil in a large salad bowl, adding extra salt and pepper to taste and the sugar if you like.

Just before serving, tip the greens into a serving bowl, drizzle over the dressing and toss everything together well.

Sift the flour into a large mixing bowl along with the ginger and allspice. Add the sugar, syrup and butter mixture and mix well until thoroughly combined.

Put just 4 teaspoonfuls of the mixture on the first baking sheet, allowing plenty of room inbetween for them to spread. Put in the preheated oven and cook for 8–10 minutes or until they are a rich brown. Five minutes later repeat with the second baking sheet. (Baking the brandy snaps in batches gives you time to roll them up while they're still warm, otherwise they'll break rather than bend.) When you remove the first batch of snaps, leave them to cool for a minute, then ease them off the paper with a palette knife.

If you want them the traditional curled-up brandy snap shape, roll them straightaway around the oiled handle of a wooden spoon, then place on a clean baking sheet to cool. Otherwise, just leave them flat. Keep baking the mixture in batches of 4 until it is all used up. The brandy snaps will keep for 2–3 days in an airtight container.

Caramelized figs with cinnamon and sweet sherry

This is a very easy way to glam up a tub of store-bought toffee or caramel ice cream.

6 fresh ripe figs
2 tablespoons soft light brown sugar
1 teaspoon ground cinnamon
1 tablespoon unsalted butter
6 tablespoons sweet oloroso sherry
caramel or toffee ice cream, to serve

a medium ovenproof dish, buttered

Serves 6

Wash the figs carefully and pat dry. Halve and lay them cut-side up in the prepared ovenproof dish. Mix the sugar and cinnamon together and sprinkle over the figs. Put a knob of butter on top of each half fig and spoon over the sherry. Place the dish on the lowest grill/broiler level and grill/broil until the butter and sugar have melted and the figs are beginning to caramelize (about 5–6 minutes). Serve with the ice cream, spooning over the warm syrup.

Brandy snaps

This is one of those clever recipes that looks incredibly difficult but is in fact quite easy to follow.

2 tablespoons golden or corn syrup
75 g/6 tablespoons soft light brown sugar
50 g/3 tablespoons unsalted butter
50 g/⅓ cup plain/all-purpose flour
½ teaspoon ground ginger
¼ teaspoon ground allspice

2 large baking sheets lined with non-stick baking parchment

Makes 12

Preheat the oven to 160°C (325°F) Gas 3. Put the syrup into a large saucepan. Add the sugar and butter and heat very gently until just melted, then take the pan off the heat. Don't allow the mixture to boil.

A Family Sunday Lunch

When several generations are involved, it's always better to play safe with the menu and stick to tried and trusted favourites like roast chicken and fruit crumbles. The good news is that these simple dishes are a great foil for fine wines – which gives the adults a treat!

Homemade cheese nibbles
Parmesan and pistachio biscuits
Cheddar crispies

*

Superlative roast chicken with sausage meatballs
Crunchy roast potatoes
Buttery peas

*

Raspberry, apple and almond crumble

*

To Drink

There's a fantastic affinity between warm cheesy biscuits and Champagne or Champagne-style sparkling wines, so that would be a great way to kick off this meal. With the roast, drink any light- or medium-bodied red wine a red Burgundy or other Pinot Noir or a Merlot-based red such as St. Emilion would be my top choices. Pair the dessert with a light, lemony Sauternes or Sauternes-style dessert wine such as Monbazillac or Saussignac or a late-harvest Sauvignon or Semillon.

Homemade cheese nibbles

It's easy enough to buy in nibbles to have with a pre-lunch drink, but it's so simple to make your own. It can also be a fun thing to do with any budding young cooks in the family. These can be made ahead and then reheated.

Parmesan and pistachio biscuits

90 g/¾ cup plain/all-purpose flour
50 g/3½ tablespoons butter, softened
50 g/½ cup finely grated mature Parmesan cheese, plus extra for topping
25 g/3 tablespoons finely chopped pistachio nuts
1 large egg yolk
½ teaspoon fine sea salt
cayenne pepper, to taste

a 7-cm/3-inch cookie cutter

a baking sheet, lightly greased

Makes about 18–20 biscuits

Preheat the oven to 190°C (375°F) Gas 5. Put the flour, butter, Parmesan, nuts and seasoning in a food processor and pulse until you have a crumbly mixture. Add the egg yolk and enough water (a teaspoon or two) to form a stiff dough. Transfer the dough to a lightly-floured work surface or board, knead lightly and roll out quite thinly. Stamp out rounds with the cookie cutter and carefully transfer them with a palate knife to the baking sheet. Re-roll the offcuts and stamp as many more biscuits as you can get out of the dough.

Sprinkle the biscuits lightly with Parmesan and bake in the preheated oven for about 15–20 minutes, until lightly browned. Leave on the baking sheet for a few minutes then transfer to a wire rack to cool for 10–15 minutes. If not eating straight away, store in an airtight container then reheat at 160°C (325°F) Gas 3 for 7–8 minutes before serving.

Cheddar crispies

110 g/¾ cup plus 2 tablespoons plain/all-purpose flour
½ teaspoon salt
110 g/1 stick butter, chilled and cut into cubes
110 g/1 cup grated mature Cheddar cheese
25 g/½ cup crisped rice cereal
sesame seeds and poppy seeds, to garnish
freshly ground black pepper

2 baking sheets, lightly greased

Makes about 20 crispies

Preheat the oven to 180°C (350°F) Gas 4. Put the flour and salt in a bowl and season with pepper. Add the cubed butter and rub in until the mixture resembles coarse breadcrumbs. Add the grated cheese and crisped rice and pull the mixture together. Take spoonfuls of the mixture and roll them into small, walnut-sized balls. Arrange on the baking sheets and flatten each ball lightly with the prongs of a fork. Sprinkle half the crispies with sesame seeds and half with poppy seeds and bake for 15–20 minutes until lightly browned. Leave on the baking sheets for a few minutes, then transfer to a wire rack to cool for 10 minutes. If not eating straight away, store in an airtight container, then reheat at 160°C (325°F) Gas 3 for 7–8 minutes before serving.

WINE RECOMMENDATION:

Serve Champagne or Champagne-style sparkling wine, which pairs wonderfully with warm, cheesy biscuits.

Superlative roast chicken with sausage meatballs

This is a simple but delicious recipe you are guaranteed to return to regularly. By cooking two small birds rather than one big one, everyone has a chance to have their favourite bit. You can make a more sophisticated unthickened wine-based gravy if you prefer, but this is the type of gravy children (and grandparents) tend to go for!

2 small–medium chickens (about 1.25 kg/3 lb.), preferably organic
1 large unwaxed lemon
2 garlic cloves, unpeeled and flattened
2 small handfuls of parsley
1 tablespoon olive oil
25 g/2 tablespoons butter
sea salt and freshly ground black pepper

For the meatballs:
450 g/1 lb. best-quality traditional pork sausages
2 tablespoons finely chopped parsley
a little plain/all-purpose flour for rolling

For the gravy:
2 tablespoons plain/all-purpose flour
400 ml/1²/₃ cup fresh chicken stock or made from 1 organic stock cube

a large roasting pan

Serves 6

Preheat the oven to 200°C (400°F) Gas 6. Grate a little zest from the lemon and reserve it for the sausage meatballs. Remove any giblets from inside the birds and stuff each of them with half a lemon, a flattened garlic clove and a small handful of parsley. Heat the olive oil gently in a saucepan, add the butter, then when it has melted brush the chickens with the oil and butter mixture. Season the birds with salt and pepper and place them in the roasting pan, breast-side upwards. Put in the preheated oven to roast for 20 minutes until the breast begins to brown. Turn the chickens on one side and roast for a further 15 minutes, while you make the sausage meatballs (these will be added to the pan and cooked with the chicken).

Slit the skins of the sausages and tip the meat into a bowl. Add the chopped parsley, lemon zest and pepper and mix well. Form into about 18 small walnut-sized balls and brown lightly on all sides in a frying pan. Carefully pour or spoon out most of the fat and juices that have accumulated in the roasting pan and reserve them. Turn the chickens onto their other side. Add the lightly browned

meatballs and cook for another 15 minutes. Finally, turn the chickens breast-side upwards again, turn the meatballs, baste the chickens with the remaining pan juices and cook for a final 10–15 minutes until the chickens are crisp and brown and fully cooked. Take the chickens and meatballs out of the oven and transfer to a warmed serving plate. Lightly cover with foil.

For the gravy, skim the fat off the reserved juices. Pour off all but 3 tablespoons of fat from the pan, stir in the flour and cook for a minute. Add the skimmed pan juices and a third of the stock and bring to the boil, stirring and scraping off any dark sticky bits from the side of the pan. Add the remaining stock, then simmer until thick (about 3–4 minutes). Check the seasoning, adding salt and pepper to taste, and strain the gravy into a warmed gravy boat.

Serve the chicken with the meatballs, roast potatoes and buttery peas or other child-friendly vegetables.

Crunchy roast potatoes

1.5 kg/3½ lb. roasting potatoes
5–6 tablespoons rapeseed or vegetable oil
sea salt

a medium roasting pan

Serves 6

Preheat the oven to 200°C (400°F) Gas 6. Peel the potatoes, halve or quarter them depending how big they are and place them in a large saucepan. Cover with cold water and bring to the boil. Add a little salt, boil for 5 minutes, then drain the potatoes. Pour the oil into a roasting pan and tip in the potatoes, turning them in the oil. Roast the potatoes in the preheated oven for 45 minutes, turning them halfway through the cooking time. Turn the heat up to 220°C (425°F) Gas 7 and continue to cook until the potatoes are crisp (about another 15–20 minutes).

Buttery peas

450 g/3 cups fresh shelled or frozen peas
a sprig of mint
40 g/2½ tablespoons butter, softened
2 tablespoons finely chopped parsley or chives (optional)

Serves 6

Put the peas in a saucepan, add the mint and cover with boiling water. Bring back to the boil and cook for about 3–5 minutes until the peas are tender. Drain, add the butter and herbs, if using, and toss together well. Serve immediately.

Raspberry, apple and almond crumble

The addition of raspberries to this otherwise traditional crumble not only gives it a gorgeous colour but creates a pleasing tartness that makes it a brilliant match with a fine dessert wine.

3 large tart apples (such as Bramley), peeled, quartered, cored and sliced

3–4 tablespoons caster/granulated sugar

250 g/9 oz. fresh or frozen raspberries

For the crumble topping:

150 g/1 cup plus 2 tablespoons plain/all-purpose flour

25 g/1 oz. ground almonds

110 g/1 stick butter, chilled and cut into cubes

50 g/¼ cup caster/granulated sugar

25 g/1 oz. flaked/slivered almonds (optional)

vanilla ice cream or cream, to serve

a shallow ovenproof dish, lightly greased

Serves 6

Put the apples in a large saucepan. Sprinkle over 3 tablespoons sugar and 3 tablespoons water. Cover the pan, place over low heat and cook for about 15 minutes, shaking the pan occasionally until the apple pieces are soft but still holding their shape. Stir in the raspberries and check for sweetness, adding a little extra sugar if it seems too sharp. Transfer to the prepared dish and let cool.

To make the topping, put the flour and ground almonds in a large bowl. Keep cutting the butter cubes into the flour mixture until you can't get the pieces any smaller, then rub the butter and flour mixture together with your fingertips until the mixture resembles coarse breadcrumbs. Stir in the sugar and carry on rubbing for another minute. Stir in the flaked/slivered almonds, if using.

When the fruit has cooled, set the oven to 200°C (400°F) Gas 6. Spread the crumble mixture evenly over the fruit, covering the whole surface, then bake for 35–40 minutes until the topping is golden. Leave to cool for 10–15 minutes before serving.

WINE RECOMMENDATION:

Any light- or medium-bodied red wine, such as a Pinot Noir or Merlot.

WINE RECOMMENDATION:

Sauternes, a late-harvest Semillon or Sauvignon, or a dessert wine such as Monbazillac or Saussignac.

Wine with Friends

Friends for Brunch

Bloody Mary granitas • Summer berries with Greek yogurt, honey and granola
Smoked salmon kedgeree • Breakfast mini-muffins: Banana and honey;
Bacon, onion and Cheddar; Spring vegetable and goats' cheese • 'Juice Bar'
St. Clement's punch • Strawberry sunrise

Tapas and Sherry

Albondigas • Spanish vegetable tortilla • Mixed seafood salad with lemon, caper
and parsley dressing • Braised beans with pancetta and mint
Spanish-style orange and almond cake

A Quick Deli Supper

Antipasti • Wild mushroom risotto • Lemon and raspberry iced vodka Martinis
Choc-mint Martinis • Banoffee Martinis

A Farmers' Market Dinner

Pea and Parma ham crostini • Farmers' market salad with goats' cheese,
asparagus and roast beets • Spring vegetable pasta with lemon
Strawberry, rose and rhubarb fool

Friends for Brunch

If you have guests staying over, brunch is the perfect relaxed weekend meal. The food needs to be light and fresh but flavourful, healthy but comforting. Kedgeree is easier than juggling a fry-up for a crowd, while the muffins can be made in advance, frozen and reheated. And the juice bar makes a fun focus to the occasion.

Bloody Mary granitas

*

Summer berries with Greek yogurt, honey and granola

*

Smoked salmon kedgeree

*

Breakfast mini-muffins: Banana and honey; Bacon, onion and Cheddar; Spring vegetable and goats' cheese

*

'Juice Bar' St. Clement's punch, Strawberry sunrise

*

To Drink

Sparkling wine is the best wine to serve at a brunch: it suits the time of day perfectly and is a great match with eggs. It needn't be Champagne: there are many good quality sparkling wines available. Mix with fresh orange juice for a refreshing Bucks Fizz.

Bloody Mary granitas

A refreshing palate cleanser to kick off or round up brunch.

7–8 tomatoes, skinned and roughly chopped

450 ml/2 cups tomato juice

100 ml/3½ fl oz. vodka

1 tablespoon Worcestershire sauce

freshly squeezed juice of 1 lime

1 teaspoon celery salt

1 teaspoon finely grated onion

sea salt, freshly ground black pepper and hot pepper sauce, such as Tabasco, to taste

a few finely snipped chives, to garnish

Makes 10–12 shots

Put the tomatoes in a food processor and whizz until smooth. Add the tomato juice and vodka and whizz again. Next, add the Worcestershire sauce, lime juice, celery salt and onion, whizz, then check the seasoning, adding salt, pepper and hot pepper sauce to taste. Pour into a shallow plastic box and freeze for about 1½ hours. Rough up the surface with a fork and freeze for another 45 minutes. Fork through again and freeze for another 45 minutes if serving straight away or freeze until hard if making ahead, in which case mellow in the fridge for 30 minutes before serving.

Spoon into shot glasses and garnish with a few finely snipped chives. Serve with coffee spoons or other small spoons.

Summer berries with Greek yogurt, honey and granola

Fill a large glass bowl with assorted fresh berries such as strawberries, raspberries, blueberries and pitted cherries. Have a big bowl of Greek or Greek-style yogurt and a smaller one of Greek honey or other flavoured clear honey alongside, together with a bowl of crunchy granola.

Smoked salmon kedgeree

Kedgeree is an Anglo-Indian dish that stems from the days of the Raj. This party version is based on a relatively new product – lightly smoked salmon, which gives it a particularly luxurious flavour. If you can't find it, use organic salmon and add a little bit of smoked salmon at the end when you add the prawns/shrimp.

3 large eggs

250 g/9 oz. undyed skinless, smoked haddock or cod fillet

250 g/9 oz. lightly smoked skinless, salmon fillet or ordinary salmon fillet

3 tablespoons sunflower oil

1 onion, finely chopped

2–3 teaspoons mild curry powder

300 g/1½ cups basmati rice

175 g/6 oz. cooked shelled prawns/shrimp

40 g/3 tablespoons butter, softened

2–3 tablespoons freshly squeezed lemon juice

3 generous tablespoons chopped coriander/cilantro leaves, plus a few whole leaves to garnish

sea salt and freshly ground black pepper

Serves 6

Bring a small saucepan of water to the boil. Prick the eggs if you have an egg pricker, lower them carefully into the water and boil for 10–12 minutes. Drain off the water, pour cold running water over the eggs, then leave to cool in cold water.

Put the haddock and salmon into a large pan and pour over just enough cold water to cover. Bring gradually to the boil, then once the water is bubbling, take the pan off the heat and cover it with a lid or a piece of foil. Leave for 5 minutes, then carefully remove the fish fillets. Pour 600 ml/2½ cups of the cooking water into a jug/pitcher and set aside.

Heat the oil in another heavy-duty pan and fry the onion over moderate heat for about 6–7 minutes until starting to turn dark brown at the edges. Sprinkle in the curry powder (Use 2 teaspoons if you would like a slightly milder flavour or 3 for a stronger flavour). Add the rice, stir again and pour in the reserved water you used for cooking the fish. Bring to the boil then turn the heat right down and cover the pan. Cook for about 15–20 minutes until all the liquid has been absorbed.

Meanwhile, shell and quarter the eggs. Set aside 6 quarters and roughly chop the rest. Flake the fish, being careful to remove any remaining bones. Once the rice is cooked, fork it through and tip in the cooked fish, prawns/shrimp and chopped eggs, cover the pan and leave for 5 minutes over very low heat. Turn off the heat, add the butter and fork through. Season to taste with the lemon juice and a little salt and pepper if you think it needs it and fork through the chopped coriander/cilantro. Serve on a warmed platter garnished with the quartered eggs and the remaining coriander/cilantro leaves.

• You can keep the kedgeree warm in a covered pan for about 15–20 minutes before serving or transfer it to a very low oven for about 30–40 minutes.

Breakfast muffins

Banana and honey mini-muffins

50 g/3 tablespoons unsalted butter
2 tablespoons clear honey
1 heaped tablespoon plain yogurt
about 60 ml/ ¼ cup milk
½ teaspoon vanilla extract
150 g/1 cup plus 2 tablespoons plain/all-purpose flour
1½ teaspoons baking powder
½ teaspoon ground cinnamon
¼ teaspoon salt
1 large egg, lightly beaten
1 medium-ripe banana
caster/superfine sugar, for topping

a 12-hole small muffin or tartlet pan lined with 12 small paper cases

Makes about 12 small muffins

Preheat the oven to 190°C (375°F) Gas 5. Gently heat the butter in a saucepan with the honey. Set aside and cool slightly. Put the yogurt in a measuring jug/pitcher and mix in enough milk to bring it to just over the 100 ml/⅓ cup mark. Stir in the vanilla extract. Sift the flour into a bowl with the baking powder, cinnamon and salt and hollow out a dip in the centre. Pour the

honey and butter mixture, beaten egg and yogurt and milk into the flour and mix in lightly and swiftly with a large metal spoon to get a rough batter. (Don't overmix – it doesn't have to be completely smooth). Peel the banana, slice it thinly into the batter and fold in lightly so that all the slices are coated. Spoon the batter into the muffin cases and sprinkle each with a little caster/superfine sugar. Bake for about 20 minutes or until risen and well browned. Transfer to a wire rack and eat as soon as cool enough to handle.

Bacon, onion and Cheddar mini-muffins

1 tablespoon sunflower or other cooking oil
75 g/2½ oz. cubed pancetta or bacon lardons
1 small onion, finely chopped
50 g/3 tablespoons unsalted butter
1 generous tablespoon plain yogurt
about 60 ml/ ¼ cup milk
150 g/1 cup plus 2 tablespoons plain/all-purpose flour
1½ teaspoons baking powder
¼ teaspoon salt
15 g/2 tablespoons grated Parmesan cheese
1 large egg, lightly beaten
40 g/⅓ cup coarsely grated Cheddar cheese

a 12-hole small muffin or tartlet pan lined with 12 small paper cases

Makes about 12 small muffins

Preheat the oven to 190°C (375°F) Gas 5. Heat the oil in a small frying pan and fry the bacon for a couple of minutes until it starts to brown. Add the onion, stir and cook over low to medium heat for another 5 minutes until the onion is soft, then set aside to cool.

Gently melt the butter in another pan and leave to cool. Put the yogurt in a measuring jug/pitcher and mix in enough milk to bring it to just over the 100 ml/⅓ cup mark. Sift the flour into a bowl with the baking powder and salt. Add the Parmesan and hollow out a dip in the centre. Pour the beaten egg, melted butter and yogurt and milk into the flour and mix in lightly and swiftly with a large metal spoon to get a rough batter. (Don't overmix – it doesn't have to be completely smooth). Fold in the bacon and onion.

Spoon the batter into the muffin cases and sprinkle each with a little grated Cheddar. Bake in the preheated oven for 20–25 minutes or until fully risen and well browned. Transfer to a wire rack and eat as soon as cool enough to handle.

Spring vegetable and goats' cheese mini-muffins

Follow the Bacon, Onion and Cheddar Mini-Muffin recipe substituting 75 g/½ cup grated courgette/zucchini, 75 g/½ cup grated mature goats' cheese and 1–2 trimmed and thinly sliced spring onions/scallions for the bacon, onion and Cheddar. (You don't need to precook the courgette/zucchini and onion, so you don't need the oil either.) Again, save some of the cheese for topping the muffins. You could also add a tablespoon of finely chopped dill to the mixture. These are better served cold rather than warm.

Juice bar

It's fun to give your guests a chance to make their own juices and smoothies. Just lay on a selection of different fruits and a blender or juicer. Combinations that go well are all kinds of citrus fruits; strawberries, orange and banana; and carrot, apple, lemon and ginger. (You could also try the Watermelon and Strawberry Cooler on page 87.)

Time-saving tip: If you don't have a juicer, buy high-quality ready-made chilled juices or smoothies and serve them in attractive glass jugs/pitchers.

St. Clement's punch

This is a fresh, zesty, citrus-based punch that's packed with vitamin C.

250 ml/1 cup freshly squeezed orange juice (about 4 oranges)
150 ml/⅔ cup freshly squeezed pink grapefruit juice (about 1–2 grapefruit)
250 ml/1 cup traditional lemonade or lemon refresher, chilled
slices of orange and lemon, to garnish

Serves 4–6

Simply pour the orange and grapefruit juice into a jug/pitcher, top up with the lemonade and stir well. Add a few slices of orange and lemon to the jug/pitcher and serve.

• If you're feeling indulgent, simply add a tablespoon of Grand Marnier. It just gives it that extra edge!

Strawberry sunrise

Technically, this is a smoothie (a mixture of fruit juice and yogurt) rather than a juice and can be made in an ordinary blender. Ideal for those who can't face solid food until lunchtime.

2 ripe bananas
200 g/1 cup fresh strawberries
freshly squeezed juice of 2 oranges
300 ml/1¼ cups plain yogurt
clear honey, to taste

Serves 2–3

Peel and slice the banana. Hull and halve the strawberries. Place both in a blender with the juice of 1 orange and whizz until smooth. Add the yogurt and honey to taste and whizz again.

Tapas and Sherry

Although this is essentially a drinks party with snacks, you can actually offer some quite substantial food – what the Spanish would refer to as 'raciones'. As with other menus, you can buy in many of the dishes from a deli – Serrano ham, Manchego cheese, marinated olives and piquillo peppers, or toasted and salted Marcona almonds – but there are some great recipes here to add to your repertoire, too.

Albondigas

*

Spanish vegetable tortilla

*

Mixed seafood salad with lemon, caper and parsley dressing

*

Braised beans with pancetta and mint

*

Spanish-style orange and almond cake

*

To Drink

A chilled fino manzanilla sherry would go well with all these savoury tapas. Alternatively, you could offer Spain's famous sparkling wine, Cava, a dry Spanish 'rosado', unoaked white Rioja or Rueda or even a Spanish beer. With the dessert, serve a sweet oloroso sherry or a sherry-based orange liqueur.

Albondigas (meatballs)

Succulent, rich meatballs are a favourite tapas. They are time consuming, but children will love helping you make them – and can eat any leftovers!

3 tablespoons Spanish extra virgin olive oil

½ bunch of spring onions/scallions, trimmed and very thinly sliced or 1 small onion, very finely chopped

3 garlic cloves, crushed

400 g/14 oz. spicy pork sausages

500 g/1 lb. lean minced/ground beef

60 g/½ cup pimento-stuffed green olives, very finely chopped

2 tablespoons very finely chopped flat leaf parsley

2–3 tablespoons plain/all-purpose flour

4–5 tablespoons sunflower or light olive oil

½ teaspoon sweet (dulce) Spanish pimentón or paprika

500 ml/2 cups passata

sea salt and freshly ground black pepper

a roasting pan or ovenproof dish

cocktail sticks/toothpicks

Serves 8

Preheat the oven to 190°C (375°F) Gas 5. Heat a large frying pan over medium heat and add 2 tablespoons of the olive oil. Fry the spring onions/scallions and 2 garlic cloves for a couple of minutes without colouring until soft and set aside. Slit and pull away the skins of the sausages, put the sausagemeat in a large bowl with the beef and mix together thoroughly. Add the softened spring onions/scallions and garlic, olives and parsley, season with salt and pepper and mix again until all the ingredients are thoroughly amalgamated.

Sprinkle some of the flour over a chopping board. Lightly flour your hands before taking generous teaspoonfuls of the meat mixture and rolling them between your palms into small meatballs. Flour your board and hands again as necessary. Wipe the frying pan with paper towels and put back on the heat. Add 3 tablespoons of the oil and fry the meatballs in batches, browning them on all sides, adding extra oil if needed. Put the meatballs in the roasting pan or ovenproof dish as you finish them.

Discard any remaining oil in the pan, rinse clean and wipe with paper towels. Replace over the heat. Add the remaining oil, garlic and the pimentón, stir for a few seconds and tip in the passata. Cook for 2–3 minutes, then check the seasoning, adding salt and pepper to taste. Pour the sauce over the meatballs and bake in the preheated oven for 35–40 minutes until they are nicely browned, turning them in the sauce halfway through the cooking time. Serve warm on cocktail sticks/toothpicks.

Spanish vegetable tortilla

Tortilla is one of those dishes that is really straightforward, but hard to make it taste as it did on your Spanish holiday. The secret is patience, as it needs much more time than a conventional omelette.

7 tablespoons Spanish extra virgin olive oil
3 medium or 2 large courgettes/zucchini, cut into slices about 1 cm/½ inch thick
350 g/12 oz. salad potatoes, very thinly sliced*
1 large Spanish onion, very thinly sliced
1 generous teaspoon finely chopped thyme (optional)
8 eggs, lightly beaten
sea salt and freshly ground black pepper

a wok

a deep-sided, non-stick frying pan about 23–24 cm/9–10 inches wide

Serves 6–8

Put 3 tablespoons of the olive oil in a wok set over medium heat and stir-fry the courgette/zucchini slices until lightly browned (about 5 minutes). Remove them from the pan with a slotted spoon, leaving behind as much of the oil as possible, and set aside. Add another 3 tablespoons of oil to the pan, heat for a minute, then tip in the potato slices and stir with a spatula to ensure they are separate and well coated with oil. Fry, stirring, for about 5–6 minutes until they start to brown, then turn the heat down, cover the pan and cook for another 10–15 minutes until the potatoes are tender, turning them every so often to ensure they don't catch. Remove them from the pan, again leaving behind as much oil as possible. Add a little more oil if necessary, then add the onion and stir-fry for about 6–7 minutes until soft and beginning to brown. Add the thyme, if using, then tip the other ingredients back into the pan, mix together lightly and season well with salt and pepper. Tip the vegetables into the beaten eggs and mix well.

Heat the smaller frying pan until moderately hot, add a little oil, wipe off the excess with paper towels, then pour in the egg mixture. Lift the vegetables up around the edge of the pan to allow the liquid egg to trickle down to the base until most of the egg is set, then turn the heat down a little and leave the tortilla to cook for about 5 minutes while you preheat the grill/broiler to moderate. Slip the pan under the grill/broiler about 12 cm/5 inches from the heat until the egg on top of the tortilla is puffed up and lightly browned and the egg in the middle has set (about another 5–6 minutes). Leave the tortilla to cool in the pan, then loosen it around the edges. Put a plate over the pan and flip the tortilla over so that it lands bottom-side upwards. Cut into wedges and serve at room temperature.

• As you slice the potatoes, put them in a bowl of cold water to get rid of the excess starch, then give them a good swirl, drain off the water and dry them with paper towels.

WINE RECOMMENDATION:

A chilled fino manzanilla sherry, Cava, a dry Spanish 'rosado' or an unoaked white Rioja or Rueda.

Mixed seafood salad with lemon, caper and parsley dressing

A mixed pack of seafood makes the basis for this easy seafood salad, which goes fabulously well with chilled manzanilla sherry.

4 tablespoons Spanish extra virgin olive oil

1 large garlic clove, crushed

500 g/1 lb. mixed seafood cocktail, thawed if frozen

150 g/5½ oz. small shelled prawns/shrimp, thawed if frozen

2 teaspoons finely grated lemon zest

1½–2 tablespoons freshly squeezed lemon juice

2 tablespoons capers, rinsed and finely chopped

3 tablespoons finely chopped flat leaf parsley

sea salt and freshly ground black pepper

Serves 6

Heat a large frying pan over medium heat, add the olive oil and garlic and fry for a few seconds, then tip in the seafood cocktail and prawns/shrimp. Turn the heat up and stir-fry for a couple of minutes so that the seafood heats right through.

Remove from the heat and add the grated lemon zest, lemon juice and capers and most of the parsley, saving a few leaves for garnishing. Mix together lightly and thoroughly. Check the seasoning adding salt and pepper to taste and extra lemon juice or olive oil if you think it needs it. Leave to cool, then cover and refrigerate for a few hours to allow the flavours to amalgamate.

Braised beans with pancetta and mint

A delicious and easy tapas that goes particularly well with the meatballs or the Spanish air-dried Serrano ham. You can obviously make this with fresh broad/fava beans in season, but the frozen ones are excellent and cut down cooking time.

3 tablespoons extra virgin olive oil

1 onion, finely chopped

65 g/2½ oz. cubed pancetta

1–2 large garlic cloves, crushed

½ teaspoon sweet (dulce) Spanish pimentón or ¼ teaspoon paprika

450 g/1 lb. frozen baby broad/fava beans

300 ml/1¼ cups hot vegetable stock

1 generous tablespoon chopped flat leaf parsley

1 generous tablespoon chopped mint leaves

sea salt and freshly ground black pepper

Serves 6–8

Heat a medium frying pan over medium heat, add 2 tablespoons of the olive oil and the onion and pancetta and fry gently for about 4–5 minutes until the onion is soft. Add the crushed garlic and pimentón, stir, then tip in the broad/fava beans. Pour in the hot stock and bring to the boil, then cook for about 10 minutes until the beans are tender.

Take off the heat, cool for about 8–10 minutes, then add the herbs and remaining olive oil. Check the seasoning, adding salt and pepper to taste. Serve at room temperature.

Spanish-style orange and almond cake

This featherlight, syrup-drenched orange and almond cake, makes an impressive finale to a tapas meal.

4 large eggs, separated

1 generous tablespoon finely grated orange zest

100 g/½ caster/superfine sugar

125 g/¾ cup ground almonds, sifted

1 teaspoon orange flower water

For the syrup:

freshly squeezed juice of 1½ oranges and 1 lemon (about 125 ml/½ cup juice in total)

75 g/6 tablespoons caster/superfine sugar

1 cinnamon stick

½ teaspoon orange flower water

a 21-cm/8-inch cake pan, lined with a round of baking parchment

Serves 8–10

Preheat the oven to 180°C (350°F) Gas 4. Put the egg yolks in a large bowl with the orange zest and all except 1 tablespoon of the sugar and beat well, until light and moussey (about 2–3 minutes). Fold in a third of the almonds, then the next third and finally the remaining third. (The mixture will be quite thick, but don't worry!) Wash and dry the beaters thoroughly. Whisk the egg whites in a separate bowl until just stiff, then add the remaining sugar and briefly whisk again. Take a couple of spoonfuls of the meringue and fold it into the cake mixture to loosen it. Fold in half the remaining meringue then, when the mixture is quite loose, carefully fold in the final portion, taking care not to overmix. Spoon the cake mixture into the prepared pan and bake for about 40–45 minutes until the surface of the cake is well browned and firm and the cake has shrunk away from the side of the pan. Remove from the oven and cool for 5 minutes, then turn out on a wire rack.

While the cake is cooking, make the syrup. Put the orange and lemon juices in a small saucepan, add the sugar, cinnamon stick and orange flower water and heat gently, stirring occasionally, until all the grains of sugar have dissolved. Bring to the boil and boil without stirring for about 4–5 minutes. Strain and cool. After the cake has cooled for about 15 minutes, put it upside-down on a plate, pierce it in several places with a skewer and spoon over some of the orange syrup, a tablespoonful at a time. Carefully turn the cake over, pierce the top of the cake and spoon over as much of the remaining syrup as the cake will absorb. Leave to finish cooling before serving.

• You can dress this up into a dinner party dessert by serving the cake with some sliced caramelized oranges and a spoonful of whipped, sweetened cream flavoured with a few drops of orange flower water.

WINE RECOMMENDATION:

Pair this intensely sweet dessert with a sweeter oloroso sherry or a sherry-based orange liqueur.

A Quick Deli Supper

Sometimes you want to have friends round midweek to share a bottle but don't have time to cook. Solution? A visit to your local deli, where you can easily source the ingredients for this simple, throw-it-together menu. All you have to do on the night is make a creamy mushroom risotto, which you can stir while you chat to your friends in the kitchen. The cocktail desserts are also a boon when you're pressed for time as they are simple and fun.

Antipasti

*

Wild mushroom risotto

*

Lemon and raspberry iced vodka Martinis, Choc-mint Martinis Banoffee Martinis

*

To Drink

Italian wines are the instinctive choice with this largely Italian-inspired menu. A dry Italian white such as a Pinot Grigio would go perfectly well with both the antipasto and the risotto. Try one from the Alto Adige in the north-east of Italy, which produces some of the best the country has to offer. Alternatively, you could switch to a supple, medium-bodied Italian red with the main course: something like a Chianti or Rosso di Montepulciano.

Antipasti

Make a colourful spread of Italian cured meats and cheeses and roasted or grilled vegetables. Take your pick from Parma ham, two different types of salami (the kind with fennel seeds is particularly delicious), mini mozzarella balls or a buffalo mozzarella and cherry tomato salad (buy some extra fresh basil to garnish), roasted peppers, courgettes/zucchini and aubergines/eggplants, grilled artichokes and marinated mushrooms. Serve with ciabatta and breadsticks.

Wild mushroom risotto

Risottos always go down well and, once you've got the hang of them, they are incredibly easy to make. Use wild mushrooms in season or chestnut/cremini mushrooms with some dried porcini when they're not available.

200 g/7 oz. wild mushrooms or 250 g/9 oz. chestnut/cremini mushrooms and 25 g/1 oz. dried porcini, soaked for 15 minutes in warm water

2 tablespoons light olive oil

90 g/6 tablespoons unsalted butter

1 small–medium onion, finely chopped

300 g/1½ cups arborio or carnaroli risotto rice

1.2 litres/5 cups homemade chicken stock or stock made with vegetable bouillon powder

125 ml/½ cup dry white wine

3 generous tablespoons Parmesan cheese, plus extra to serve

salt and freshly ground black pepper

Serves 4

Clean the fresh mushrooms by lightly brushing or wiping them with a damp cloth. Slice them thinly. If you're using porcini drain them and slice them too. Heat a medium frying pan, add 1 tablespoon of oil and 40 g/3 tablespoons of the butter and briefly fry the fresh mushrooms until lightly browned. Heat the remaining oil and 25 g/1½ tablespoons of the remaining butter in a large saucepan then add the onion. Stir and cook over a medium heat, for about 3 minutes, then tip in the rice and stir. Let it cook for about 3 minutes without colouring, stirring occasionally so that it doesn't burn. Meanwhile, heat the stock in another saucepan until it is almost boiling and leave over low heat. Pour the wine into the rice. It will sizzle and evaporate almost immediately. Add the dried mushrooms, if using, then gradually add the stock, a ladleful at a time, stirring the risotto in between and cooking it until the liquid has almost been absorbed. Then add the next lot of stock and repeat until the rice is nice and creamy but still has a little 'bite' to it. This will take about 20 minutes. About 5 minutes before the end of the cooking time, stir in the sautéed mushrooms, leaving a few for garnishing. When the risotto is ready, stir in the remaining butter and Parmesan and season to taste with salt and pepper. Leave the pan covered for a few minutes while you reheat the remaining mushrooms. Serve the risotto in bowls topped with a few mushrooms and some extra Parmesan. Serve with a rocket/arugula salad.

WINE RECOMMENDATION:

Pair the risotto with the Pinot Grigio, or switch to a supple, medium-bodied Italian red, such as a Chianti or Montepulciano.

Dessert cocktails

Easy, light, stunning. Iced vodka Martinis are the perfect midweek dessert, so long as you don't have too many of them! Ultra-sweet, creamy cocktails also make a brilliant instant dessert, so try these too.

Lemon and raspberry iced vodka Martinis

500 ml/1 pint lemon sorbet
500 ml/1 pint raspberry sorbet
4 shots of frozen* vodka

4 Martini glasses, frosted in the freezer

Makes 4 drinks

Take the sorbets out of the freezer 20 minutes before you want to serve them and transfer to the fridge. Scoop a couple of balls of sorbet into each glass (same flavour or mixed) and pour over a splash of vodka.

• Vodka won't actually freeze but keep the bottle in the freezer and it will be wonderfully cold.

Choc-mint Martinis

4 scoops chocolate mint ice cream
4 shots chilled or frozen vodka
2 shots coffee-flavoured liqueur,
such as Kahlúa
cocoa powder, to garnish

4 Martini glasses, frosted in the freezer

Makes 4 drinks

Put the ice cream in a blender with the vodka and coffee-flavoured liqueur. Whizz until smooth then try the blend, adjusting the proportions of ice cream, vodka or liqueur to taste. Pour into the glasses and sift a little cocoa powder over the surface, to garnish.

Banoffee Martinis

1 ripe banana, sliced
ice cubes
3 shots vanilla-flavoured vodka or ordinary vodka and a few drops of vanilla extract
2 shots toffee- or caramel-flavoured liqueur
2 shots milk
a small pinch of ground nutmeg (optional)
powdered drinking chocolate, to garnish

2 Martini glasses, frosted in the freezer

Makes 2 drinks

Whizz the banana in a blender with the vodka. Tip the purée into a shaker full of ice cubes. Add the toffee liqueur, milk and nutmeg, if using, and shake vigorously. Strain into the glasses and sift a little chocolate powder over the surface.

A Farmers' Market Dinner

There's nothing more inspirational than a visit to the local farmers' market, especially in spring when the new season's vegetables finally arrive after the bleak stretch of winter. Invite friends round to share the bounty the same evening and enjoy the produce at its freshest and best.

Pea and Parma ham crostini

*

Farmers' market salad with goats' cheese, asparagus and roast beets

*

Spring vegetable pasta with lemon

*

Strawberry, rose and rhubarb fool

*

To Drink

At this time of year, keep the drink light and white. The green sappy, citrussy flavours of Sauvignon Blanc are a perfect choice with the first two courses of this menu. Choose one from the Loire like a Sancerre or Pouilly Fumé. With the pasta, serve a good Italian Pinot Grigio or a Chablis. You could offer non-drinkers an elderflower spritzer.

Pea and Parma ham crostini

The new season's peas are so deliciously sweet that you want to enjoy them every which way you can.

250 g/2 cups shelled fresh or frozen peas
2 spring onions/scallions
40 g/⅓ cup finely grated aged pecorino or Parmesan cheese
1 tablespoon finely chopped mint or dill
2 tablespoons fruity olive oil
18 ciabatta toasts (see page 70)
125 g/4½ oz. thinly sliced Parma ham or other air-dried ham, torn or cut in half
salt and freshly ground black pepper
freshly squeezed lemon juice, to taste

Makes 18 crostini

Cook the peas in boiling water for 2–3 minutes or until just tender. Drain under cold running water. Trim and cut the spring onions/scallions in half lengthways, then slice very thinly.

Put the peas and spring onions/scallions in a food processor and pulse until you get a chunky spread. Add the pecorino and mint and pulse again, then stir in the olive oil. Season to taste with salt, pepper and lemon juice. Spread the mixture thickly on ciabatta toasts and drape with a piece of ham. Serve immediately.

Farmers' market salad with goats' cheese, asparagus and roast beets

Don't let memories of vinegar-soused beetroot put you off – roast beetroot has a fabulously sweet, earthy flavour that just needs a few salad leaves and some fresh tangy white goats' cheese to set it off perfectly.

a bunch of fresh beet(root)
4 tablespoons sunflower oil
800 g/2 lb. broad/fava bean pods
a bunch of fresh asparagus
3 tablespoons rice vinegar
2 tablespoons walnut oil
100 g/2 generous handfuls mixed salad leaves, such as rocket/arugula, watercress, baby spinach or mustard leaves
200 g/7 oz. goats' cheese
a small handful of chopped green herbs, such as parsley or dill
a few chives, snipped
sea salt and freshly ground black pepper

Serves 4–6

Preheat the oven to 200°C (400°F) Gas 6. Cut off the beet(root) tops and trim off the roots. Wash the beet(root) under running water to remove any dirt and dry with paper towels. Take a large piece of foil and place it on a baking sheet. Oil it lightly, place the beet(root) in the centre and scrunch the edges of the foil together to make a loose tent. Cook in the preheated oven for about 50 minutes–1 hour, or until tender. When cool enough to handle, peel off the skins and cut into quarters or smaller wedges.

Meanwhile, pod the broad/fava beans and cook them in a pan of boiling water for about 8–10 minutes or until just cooked. When cool enough to handle, pop the beans out of their skins. Cut the tips of the asparagus off about a third of the way down the stalk and steam or microwave for about 3–4 minutes until just tender. Set aside and let cool.

Shake the vinegar, oils, salt and pepper together in a screw-top glass jar. Use half to lightly dress the beet(root). Divide the leaves between 4 plates and drizzle with a little of the remaining dressing. Arrange the beet(root) wedges over the leaves and top with roughly torn chunks of goats' cheese and the beans. Sprinkle over the herbs and the remaining dressing and grind a little black pepper over the top. Serve with some crusty bread.

WINE RECOMMENDATION:

A Sauvignon Blanc, preferably one from the Loire such as a Sancerre or Pouilly Fumé.

Spring vegetable pasta with lemon

This dish is admittedly more vegetable than pasta, but it's one of the most delicious ways to enjoy the new season's produce. You can vary the vegetables depending on what's available. Baby courgettes/zucchini also work well, as does fennel. The key thing is to cook them until they're only just done to preserve their delicate flavour and bright green colour.

a small bunch of asparagus
150 g/1 cup shelled fresh peas
a few stalks of sprouting broccoli
150 g/5½ oz. shelled broad/fava beans
110 g/1 stick butter
1 leek or ½ bunch of spring onions/scallions, thinly sliced
300 ml/1¼ cups double/heavy cream
300 g/10½ oz. dried egg pasta shapes, such as Campanelle
freshly squeezed juice of 2–3 lemons (about 125 ml/½ cup)
3 generous tablespoons finely chopped parsley
2 generous tablespoons each finely chopped dill and chives
sea salt and freshly ground black pepper
freshly shaved Parmesan cheese or grana padano, to serve

Serves 6

Snap the asparagus spears two-thirds down the stalks and discard the woody ends. Cut the remaining stem into short lengths. Steam or microwave them for about 2–3 minutes until just cooked and refresh with cold water. Repeat with the other vegetables – steaming them individually until just cooked. (Pop the broad/fava beans out of their skins for an even sweeter taste).

Gently melt the butter in a large saucepan or flameproof casserole and cook the leek for a couple of minutes until starting to soften. Tip in the other vegetables, lightly toss with the butter, cover the pan and leave over very low heat, adding the cream once the vegetables have heated through.

Cook the pasta following the instructions on the package. Reserve a little of the cooking water and drain well. Tip the drained pasta into the vegetables and toss together. Add the lemon juice and herbs, season with salt and pepper and toss together lightly. Check the seasoning, adding extra salt, pepper, lemon juice or a little of the reserved pasta cooking water to lighten the sauce if you think it needs it. Serve in warm bowls with shavings of Parmesan.

WINE RECOMMENDATION:

A good Italian Pinot Grigio, or a Chablis. Elderflower spritzers make a good non-alcoholic alternative.

Strawberry, rose and rhubarb fool

Rhubarb and strawberries have an extraordinary affinity, which is fortunate as they come into season at the same time of year. Add a hint of rose and a light cream, and you have a simple but impressive dessert.

400 g/14 oz. fresh rhubarb
3 tablespoons caster/superfine sugar
225 g/1½ cups fresh, ripe strawberries, plus a few extra to garnish
2–3 tablespoons rose syrup or rosewater and extra caster/superfine sugar
300 g/1¼ cups Greek yogurt
300 g/1¼ cups whipping cream

6 glasses or glass serving dishes

Serves 6

Slice the rhubarb and put it in a saucepan with the sugar and 2 tablespoons water. Put a lid on the pan and heat over low heat until the fruit comes to the boil, then turn the heat down and simmer for 7–10 minutes until the fruit is soft. Tip the fruit into a sieve/strainer over a bowl and drain off the juice.

Hull all the strawberries, put all but those reserved for the garnish in a food processor and whizz until smooth. Add the drained rhubarb and 1 tablespoon rose syrup or 2 teaspoons rosewater with 1 tablespoon caster/superfine sugar and whizz again. Tip the purée into a bowl and leave to cool.

Put the yogurt into a large bowl. In a separate bowl, whip the cream until just holding its shape and sweeten to taste with rose syrup or rosewater and sugar. Fold half the rose cream into the yogurt followed by half of the puréed strawberry and rhubarb, to form a base. Add the remaining cream and the rest of the rhubarb and strawberry purée and fold in gently to create a pretty marbled effect, being careful not to overmix.

Spoon the fool into individual glasses and chill until ready to serve. Slice the remaining strawberries and sprinkle with a few drops of rose syrup or a little sugar. Use the strawberry slices to decorate the top of each glass.

Time-saving tip: If you don't have time to make a dessert, simply serve some early-season strawberries with pouring cream. You'll probably need to sweeten them a touch at this time of year: slice a sprinkle them with sugar then leave them to macerate for 15–20 minutes before serving them.

Special Occasions

A Romantic Champagne Dinner

Warm scallop salad with crispy pancetta and parsnip crisps • Lobster with chips/fries • Passion fruit pavlovas • Chaource with black truffle

A Festive celebration

Chestnut and puy lentil soup with whipped celeriac cream
Winter cheeseboard • Roast pumpkin and pecan pie • Ginger and cinnamon cookies • Orange-mulled wine

A Fine Wine Dinner

Potted shrimp • Roast fillet of beef with soy and butter sauce • Roast new potatoes with garlic and rosemary • Roast pears with sweet wine, honey and pine nuts • Chocolates, coffee and cognac

A Celebration Tea Party

Mini choux puffs with crab • Strawberry and mascarpone tartlets • Rose petal cupcakes • Pink cava and strawberry jellies • Raspberry and brown sugar meringues • Old-fashioned white wine cup

A Chinese New Year Supper

Sesame prawn toasts and other dim sum • Luxury seafood stir-fry • Stem ginger and almond ice cream, mandarin oranges and fortune cookies

A Romantic Champagne Dinner

The key to a romantic dinner is not to give yourself too much last-minute work or to eat and drink too much – unless you want to end up snoring on the sofa! Since you're probably going to open a bottle of Champagne at some point, you might as well drink it all the way through, which works well with this luxurious seafood-based menu.

Warm scallop salad with crispy pancetta and parsnip crisps

*

Lobster and chips

*

Passion fruit pavlovas

*

Chaource with black truffles

*

To Drink

This menu is designed to be accompanied by Champagne and, if you can run to it, a vintage one. Choose a recent vintage rather than a very old one, as you may not like the complex yeasty flavours that mature Champagne acquires. An alternative would be to drink a glass of fizz with the oysters or scallops and move on to a top-quality Chardonnay with the lobster.

Warm scallop salad with crispy pancetta and parsnip crisps

Scallops are perfect for a romantic feast: luxurious but also quick and easy to cook so there's more time to relax together. Try and buy diver-caught ones if you are able to find them.

1 parsnip
6 large fresh scallops
1 tablespoon olive oil plus a little extra for dressing the salad
60 g/2½oz. cubed pancetta
4 tablespoons full-bodied dry white wine, such as a Chardonnay or Viognier
2 tablespoons fish stock or water

1 tablespoon double/heavy cream or crème fraîche
a small bag of mixed leaf salad
sea salt and freshly ground black pepper
vegetable oil, for frying

a wok

Serves 2

First make the parsnip crisps. Peel the parsnip and cut off the bottom end to leave you with a piece about 10 cm/4 inches long and 3–4 cm/1–1½ inches wide at its narrowest point. Shave off fine slices using a mandoline or vegetable peeler. Fill a wok about one-quarter full with vegetable oil and heat until very hot. Fry the parsnip crisps in batches, a few at a time, removing them as they brown with a slotted spoon and drain them on paper towels. Sprinkle them lightly with salt.

Season the scallops on both sides with salt and black pepper. Heat a frying pan and add the olive oil. Fry the pancetta until crisp, then remove it from the pan with a slotted spoon and pour off the fat. Return the frying pan to the hob, reheat for a minute until almost smoking, then lay the scallops in the pan. Cook them for 1–1½ minutes, depending how thick they are, then turn them over and cook for the same amount of time the other side. Set aside and keep warm. Pour the white wine into the pan, let it bubble up and reduce it by half. Add the fish stock and keep bubbling away until you have just over a couple of tablespoons of juice altogether. Return any juices that have accumulated under the scallops to the pan and stir in the cream. Check the seasoning, adding pepper to taste and a little more salt if necessary, warm through for a few seconds, then turn off the heat.

Put half the salad leaves on each plate and scatter over the pancetta. Drizzle with a little olive oil and season lightly. Arrange the most attractive parsnip crisps over the top. Lay 3 scallops on each plate and spoon the pan juices over them. Serve immediately.

WINE RECOMMENDATION:

A Champagne would be a perfect accompaniment to this elegant appetizer. Go for a vintage one if you can afford to.

FOOD & FIZZ:

Sparkling wine is much more versatile with food than people think, its natural carbonation acting as a palate cleanser and appetite stimulant. Its lightness makes it a natural partner for raw or lightly cooked shellfish and other seafood, for light pastas and risottos, and with chicken. Surprisingly, although it is regarded as a dry wine, you can also drink it with airy desserts such as gâteaux, soufflés and meringues, and with red berry fruits such as strawberries and raspberries. You can also drink it with light creamy cheeses such as Chaource.

Lobster and chips/fries

Since wrestling with a live lobster is possibly not the most relaxing prelude to a romantic evening, you may wish to buy a cooked one!

1 medium–large cooked lobster
60 g/4 tablespoons butter
2 garlic cloves, crushed
2 tablespoons freshly squeezed lime juice
1 teaspoon grated fresh ginger
14–16 basil leaves, finely shredded
sea salt and cayenne pepper
hand-cut chips/fries, to serve

lobster crackers or mallet

Serves 2

Put the lobster underside downwards on a chopping board and cut through it vertically with a large sharp knife. Carefully extract the white lobster meat from the tail, removing the long, thin membrane near the back. Remove the claws and crack them with lobster crackers or hit them smartly with a mallet. Carefully remove the meat, breaking it up as little as possible. Pick out any remaining white meat from the shell, scrape out the rest and discard. Cut the lobster meat into large chunks.

Melt the butter gently in a saucepan and stir in the garlic, lime juice and ginger. Add the lobster pieces and warm through gently for a minute or 2. Add the basil and season with salt and cayenne pepper. Carefully transfer the empty shells to the baking dish and reassemble the lobster meat in the shells. Put the dish under a preheated hot grill/broiler for 2–3 minutes until you can hear the lobster meat begin to sizzle.

Serve with a few hand-cut chips/fries or baby new potatoes.

WINE RECOMMENDATION:

If you wish to move on from Champagne, try a top-quality Chardonnay with the lobster.

Passion fruit pavlovas

A simple-to-assemble, fresh-tasting and impressive dessert.

2 passion fruit
1 tablespoon freshly squeezed orange juice
1 teaspoon caster/superfine sugar, plus extra to taste
a few drops of orange flower water (optional)
2 store-bought meringue nests
2 generous tablespoons lemon or orange curd (optional)
4 small scoops good-quality vanilla ice cream

Serves 2

Halve the passion fruit and scoop the pulp and seeds into a small bowl, taking care not to remove any of the bitter pith.

Add the orange juice and sugar and stir. Check for sweetness, adding the orange flower water and/or extra sugar to taste.

Put a meringue nest on each plate and spoon the curd, if using, into the base. Top with the vanilla ice cream and spoon over the orange and passion fruit sauce.

Chaource with black truffle

If you don't wish to serve a whole cheese board for just the two of you, try this tip for a truly special finish to your meal. Take a small, deep, round, soft white rinded cows' cheese, about 7 cm/3 inches in diameter and about 4–5 cm/1½–2 inches deep or half a slightly bigger one, such as Chaource (which comes from the Champagne region of France), and cut it horizontally into three slices (this is easier if it's chilled). Thinly slice a black truffle, lay the slices between the layers, trickling over a few drops of black truffle-infused oil over the sliced truffles, and sandwich the layers together. Wrap tightly with clingfilm/plastic wrap and refrigerate for at least a day and preferably two days. Cut into wedges, bring to room temperature and serve with slices of sourdough or baguette.

A Festive Celebration

Most of us have tried and trusted recipes for our Christmas or Thanksgiving dinner, but there are many other meals to be catered for during the holiday season, and they needn't be as time consuming to prepare as The Big Meal itself. You can mix and match the courses any way you like, or simply invite a few friends round for some mulled wine and cookies.

Chestnut and Puy lentil soup
with whipped celeriac cream

*

Winter cheeseboard – see page 50

*

Roast pumpkin and pecan pie

*

Ginger and cinnamon cookies
Orange-mulled wine

*

To Drink

To match with the soup, choose a light unoaked Chardonnay, such as Chablis, or a neutral clean white, such as Albariño. (If you don't make the celeriac topping, you could use a richer, oakier Chardonnay.) Muscats and Moscatels go particularly well with pumpkin pie – try Australian liqueur Muscat if you have an exceptionally sweet tooth, or a lighter Southern French or Spanish Muscat if you haven't. You could also go for a sweet sherry or a young tawny port.

Chestnut and Puy lentil soup with whipped celeriac cream

This is a spectacularly rich, satisfying soup with a light-as-air, foamy topping. You can prepare the soup ahead and it's a particularly good way to use up a tasty turkey or ham stock. You don't have to peel your own chestnuts, but they do taste wonderful and it's a nice, cosy thing to do if you've got company in the kitchen. If you prefer to serve the soup on its own without the topping, save some of the chopped chestnut for garnishing, frying the pieces in a little butter before serving.

450 g/1 lb. whole chestnuts or 350 g/12 oz. ready-prepared chestnuts

4 tablespoons light olive oil

1 leek, trimmed and thinly sliced

1 large carrot, finely diced

1 celery stalk, thinly sliced

1 garlic clove, crushed

1 teaspoon sweet (dulce) pimentón or paprika

1.5–1.75 litres/quarts fresh turkey, duck, ham, chicken or game stock or stock made with 2 organic beef or chicken cubes

175 g/1 cup green Puy lentils, rinsed

2 tablespoons dry Marsala, Madeira or amontillado sherry

½–1 teaspoon Worcestershire or dark soy sauce (optional)

sea salt and freshly ground black pepper

For the celeriac cream:

500 g/1 lb. celeriac

568 ml/2⅓ cups semi-skimmed milk

freshly grated nutmeg, to taste

a few snipped chives, to garnish

Serves 6–8

Wash the chestnuts and make a cut with a sharp knife in the curved side of each one. Put in a saucepan of boiling water, bring back to the boil and boil for 3 minutes. Turn the heat off and remove the chestnuts 2 at a time, letting them cool for a few seconds, then peeling off both the hard outer shell and inner brown papery skin. If they become harder to peel, bring the water back to the boil again. Chop the chestnuts roughly.

Heat the oil in a large saucepan, add the leek, carrot and celery, stir well and cook over medium heat until the vegetables start to soften (about 5–6 minutes). Stir in the garlic and pimentón and cook for a minute, then add the chestnuts and 1 litre/quart of the stock and bring to the boil. Add the lentils to the vegetables, then cook for 35–40 minutes until the vegetables are soft. Cool for 10 minutes, then purée, in batches, in a food processor. Return the soup and remaining stock to the pan, add the Marsala and reheat gently. Season to taste with salt, pepper and Worcestershire sauce.

Meanwhile, to make the celeriac cream, remove the tough outer skin from the celeriac and cut it into cubes. Put in a saucepan, add enough of the milk to cover and bring to the boil. Partially cover the pan and simmer for about 20–25 minutes, until the celeriac is soft. Remove the celeriac with a slotted spoon, leaving the liquid behind, and whizz it in a food processor. Season with salt, pepper and a little freshly grated nutmeg. Remove half the purée and add half the remaining milk to the purée in the food processor. Whizz until smooth, light and foamy, adding the extra milk if needed.

Serve the soup in bowls with a generous swirl of celeriac purée on the top and garnish with snipped chives. Serve with some crusty sourdough or multigrain bread.

WINE RECOMMENDATION:

A light unoaked Chardonnay such as Chablis, or try a neutral clean white, such as Albariño.

Roast pumpkin and pecan pie

This recipe may look slightly daunting, but it is well worth the effort. Do roast the pumpkin if you're cooking it from scratch – it has a much better texture than when you boil it.

For the pastry:
250 g/2 cups plain/all-purpose flour
1 teaspoon ground ginger
2 tablespoons icing/confectioners' sugar
110 g/1 stick butter, chilled and cut into cubes
25 g/2 tablespoons white vegetable fat or shortening
1 egg yolk (reserve the white)
a pinch of salt

For the pumpkin purée:
500 g/1 lb. roast pumpkin flesh (see method)
1 tablespoon bourbon or dark rum
1 tablespoon light muscovado sugar
¼ teaspoon mixed spice
15 g/1 tablespoon butter, chilled

For the pie filling:
100 g/½ cup light muscovado sugar
1 tablespoon maple syrup
1½ teaspoons mixed/apple pie spice
½ teaspoon ground cinnamon
a pinch of salt
1 tablespoon bourbon or dark rum
3 eggs
2 tablespoons plain/self-raising flour, sifted
150 ml/2/3 cup double/heavy cream

For the pie topping:
50 g/1/3 cup pecan nuts, finely chopped
1 tablespoon light muscovado sugar

a 23-cm x 3.5 cm deep/9-inch x 1½ inch deep flan pan or pie plate

Serves 6

First make the pastry. Sift the flour, ginger and icing/confectioners' sugar into a large bowl. Cut the butter cubes and fat into the flour, then rub lightly with your fingertips until the mixture resembles coarse breadcrumbs. Mix the egg yolk with 2 tablespoons ice-cold water, add to the bowl, mix lightly and pull into a ball, adding extra water if needed. Shape into a disc, put in a plastic bag and refrigerate for at least half an hour.

Preheat the oven to 200°C (400°F) Gas 6. To make the pumpkin purée, scrape away all the pumpkin seeds and flesh surrounding them and cut into chunks. Put the chunks on a piece of lightly oiled foil. Sprinkle over the bourbon, sugar and mixed spice and dot with the chilled butter. Bring the foil up round the sides and fold over to form a loose but airtight package. Place in a baking dish and cook in the preheated oven for 40 minutes until the pumpkin is soft. Open up the foil, let cool for a few minutes, then tip the pumpkin and the juices into a food processor and whizz until smooth.

Roll out the pastry and lower into the flan pan. Trim the edges. Prick lightly with a fork and chill for another half an hour. Cover the pastry case with foil and baking beans. Bake at 200°C (400°F) Gas 6 for about 12 minutes, then remove the foil and beans, brush the base of the pastry with the reserved egg white and return to the oven for 3–4 minutes. Remove it from the oven and lower the temperature to 190°C (375°F) Gas 5.

Add the sugar and maple syrup to the pumpkin purée, then the spices, salt and bourbon. Add the eggs, one by one, beating them in well, then sift in the flour and mix lightly. Finally, add the cream and pour the filling into the pastry crust. Put the pan on a baking sheet, transfer to the oven and bake for about 50 minutes until the filling is just set and firm, reducing the temperature to 180°C (350°F) Gas 4 after 25 minutes.

About 10 minutes before the end of the cooking time, put the pecans in a saucepan with the sugar and warm gently until the sugar starts to melt. About 5 minutes before the tart is cooked, sprinkle the nuts evenly over the surface of the tart and return it to the oven for 5 minutes. Remove from the oven and let cool for 20 minutes before cutting. Serve lukewarm with lightly whipped cream.

WINE RECOMMENDATION:

A Muscat or Moscatel would pair well with this rich pie. You could also try a sweet sherry or young tawny port.

Ginger and cinnamon cookies

It's easy enough to buy Christmassy cookies, but it's worth baking them yourself if only for the gorgeous smell that permeates the kitchen. This recipe is adapted from one in an old cookery book called *Cooking for Christmas* by Shona Crawford Poole, first published in 1980.

90 g/½ cup dark muscovado sugar

110 g/1 stick soft butter, cut into cubes

6 tablespoons golden/corn syrup

100 ml/6 tablespoons double/heavy cream

375 g/3 cups plus 2 tablespoons plain/all-purpose flour

1 tablespoon ground ginger

1 tablespoon ground cinnamon

⅛ teaspoon ground cloves (optional)

1 teaspoon baking powder

½ teaspoon salt

2 baking sheets, lined with baking parchment

star-shaped cookie cutters in various sizes (or any other shapes you like, such as Christmas trees, bells etc).

Makes about 40 biscuits

Sift the sugar through a sieve/strainer to remove any lumps and put in a bowl with the cubed butter. Beat together until smooth, then beat in the golden/corn syrup and cream. Measure out the flour, add the spices, baking powder and salt and sift into another bowl. Add the flour and spice mixture to the creamed mixture a third at a time until you have a stiff dough. Form the dough into a flat disc, wrap in kitchen foil and refrigerate for at least 3 hours.

When you're ready to bake the cookies preheat the oven to 190°C (375°F) Gas 5. Cut off a quarter of the dough, flour your work surface and rolling pin generously and roll out the dough thinly. Stamp out shapes with your cutters. Carefully prise them off the work surface with a palette knife, lay them on one of the baking sheets and bake for about 8 minutes. Leave them to firm up for 2–3 minutes, then transfer to a wire rack until crisp. Repeat with the remaining pieces of dough, re-rolling the offcuts to make more cookies. The cookies will keep in an airtight container for up to one week.

Orange-mulled wine

If you've never made mulled wine yourself, you should try. It couldn't be simpler and tastes infinitely better than the ready-mixed versions. The only thing you have to be careful about is that the wine doesn't boil.

2 bottles of medium-bodied fruity red wine

1 orange studded with cloves, plus a few orange slices to serve

thinly pared zest of ½ an unwaxed lemon

2 cinnamon sticks

6 cardamom pods, lightly crushed

a little freshly grated nutmeg or a small pinch of ground nutmeg

100 g/½ cup soft brown sugar

100 ml/6 tablespoons orange-flavoured liqueur, such as Cointreau or Grand Marnier, or brandy

Makes 14–16 small cups or glasses

Pour the wine into a large saucepan and add 500 ml/2 cups cold water along with the orange, lemon zest, spices and sugar. Heat the wine gently until it is almost boiling, then turn it down to the lowest heat and leave to simmer for half an hour to allow the spices to infuse thoroughly. Add the liqueur then reheat gently. Strain the mulled wine into a large, warmed bowl and float a few thin slices of orange on top. Ladle into small cups or glasses and serve with mince pies.

A Fine Wine Dinner

Sometimes the starting point for a menu is a bottle – or bottles – of special wine. You may feel you have to pull all the culinary stops out – but don't! Nothing suits fine wines better than simple food. A delicate seafood starter, a prime cut of meat, a classic dessert – there's nothing here that's too complicated or that could clash with a treasured bottle. Let the wine be the hero.

Potted shrimp

*

Roast fillet of beef with soy and butter sauce

Roast new potatoes with garlic and rosemary

*

Roast pears with sweet wine, honey and pine nuts

*

Chocolates, coffee and cognac

*

To Drink

Potted prawns are a good match for good white Burgundy or other mature Chardonnay, so you could start with that. The gentle flavours of the meat sauce won't overwhelm an older red wine, so this is the occasion to bring out an aged bottle of Bordeaux, Burgundy, Barolo or a Rioja Gran Reserva that you have been saving for a special occasion. The dessert is the perfect excuse to crack open a bottle of Sauternes. Serve it well chilled in small glasses.

Potted prawns

Don't be tempted to use showy tiger prawns for this. The small, sweet ones have much more flavour and suit the dish better.

450 g/1 lb. cooked, shelled North Atlantic prawns/Maine shrimp, thawed if frozen
200 g/1 stick plus 5 tablespoons unsalted butter, cut into cubes
½ teaspoon ground mace
¼ teaspoon cayenne pepper or hot (piquante) pimentón
a good pinch of sea salt
1 generous tablespoon finely chopped parsley
a handful of watercress salad, to garnish
wholemeal/whole-wheat or Granary toast, to serve

6 ramekins

Serves 6

Drain the prawns/shrimp thoroughly. Melt the butter very slowly in a medium saucepan. Carefully skim off the milky-looking white layer that will have come to the surface, then mix in the mace and cayenne pepper, adding a little extra to taste if you think it needs it.

Tip the prawns/shrimp into the butter, mix in well and leave over very low heat for 15 minutes without boiling to allow the flavours to infuse. Take off the heat, add the salt (rub the flakes between your fingers) and stir in the parsley. Spoon the prawns/shrimp into the ramekins and pour over the remaining melted butter. Press the prawns/shrimp down firmly with the back of a teaspoon so as much as possible of the prawns/shrimp are submerged. Cover the dishes with clingfilm/plastic wrap and refrigerate for at least a couple of hours or preferably overnight.

Take out of the fridge 15 minutes before serving. Place each ramekin on a small plate and serve with toasted wholemeal/whole-wheat or Granary bread.

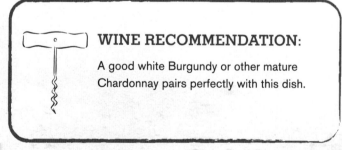

WINE RECOMMENDATION:

A good white Burgundy or other mature Chardonnay pairs perfectly with this dish.

Roast fillet of beef with soy and butter sauce

The soy and butter sauce may sound unconventional, but it makes a very light, savoury, meaty sauce that is much more wine friendly than some of the very intense winey reductions you get in restaurants.

1 teaspoon coarse sea salt

2 teaspoons black peppercorns

½ teaspoon ground allspice

1 tablespoon plain/all-purpose flour

1–1.1 kg/18–20 oz. flllet of beef

1 tablespoon sunflower or light olive oil

40 g/3 tablespoons soft butter

2 tablespoons Madeira or dry Marsala

375 ml/1½ cups fresh beef stock or stock made with ¾ organic, low-salt beef stock cube

1½ tablespoons Japanese soy sauce, such as Kikkoman

a cast-iron casserole or deep roasting pan

Serves 6

Preheat the oven to 220°C (425°F) Gas 7. Put the coarse salt and peppercorns in a mortar and grind with a pestle until finely ground. Mix in the allspice and flour. Remove any fat or sinew from the beef fillet and dry thoroughly with paper towels. Put the seasoning and flour on a plate and roll the beef in the mixture, patting it evenly into the surface and shaking off any excess. Put the casserole or roasting pan over medium to high heat, add the oil and half the butter and brown the beef quickly on all sides. Transfer to the preheated oven and roast for 20–40 minutes, depending how thick your beef fillet is and how rare you like it. Remove from the oven and set aside for 10–15 minutes, lightly covered with foil. Pour off any excess fat in the pan, leaving about 1 tablespoon. Pour in the Madeira and let it bubble up for a few seconds, then add the stock and soy sauce. Bring to the boil, turn the heat down a little and reduce by half. Pour any juices that have accumulated under the meat into the pan, whisk in the remaining butter and season with black pepper (you shouldn't need any salt).

Carve the meat into thick slices and serve on warmed plates with the sauce spooned over and served with some roast new potatoes (see right) and green beans.

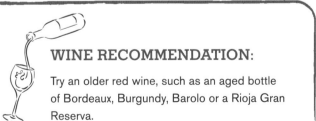

WINE RECOMMENDATION:

Try an older red wine, such as an aged bottle of Bordeaux, Burgundy, Barolo or a Rioja Gran Reserva.

Roast new potatoes with garlic and rosemary

1 kg/2¼ lb. even-sized small new potatoes

1 litre/4 cups vegetable stock made with organic vegetable stock cube or 4 teaspoons vegetable bouillon powder

2 tablespoons olive oil

3 garlic cloves, unpeeled

2–3 sprigs of rosemary

sea salt flakes

a roasting dish

Serves 6

Preheat the oven to 220°C (425°F) Gas 7. Scrub the potatoes well and put in a saucepan. Cover with the boiling vegetable stock, bring back to the boil and cook for about 5–6 minutes. Drain well and tip into a roasting dish. Pour over the olive oil and toss the potatoes so that they are evenly coated. Crush the garlic cloves lightly, distribute them around the dish, together with the sprigs of rosemary. Toss again and roast in the preheated oven for about 20–25 minutes until nicely browned, turning the potatoes halfway through. Discard the garlic and rosemary, sprinkle the potatoes with salt flakes and serve.

Roast pears with sweet wine, honey and pine nuts

Roasting pears in wine transforms them from everyday fruit into a light but luxurious dessert. The trick is to use an inexpensive wine for cooking and a better wine of the same type to serve with it.

freshly squeezed juice of 1 lemon (about 3 tablespoons)
9 just-ripe, small Conference pears
50 g/3 tablespoons butter, softened
3 tablespoons fragrant honey
175 ml/⅔ cup Premières Côtes de Bordeaux or late-harvested Sauvignon or Semillon
50 g/⅓ cup pine nuts
2 teaspoons caster/granulated sugar
200 ml/¾ cup double/heavy cream
2 teaspoons vanilla sugar or ½ teaspoon vanilla extract and 2 teaspoons caster/granulated sugar

a large roasting pan or ovenproof dish (large enough to take the pears in a single layer), well buttered

Serves 6

Preheat the oven to 190°C (375°F) Gas 5. Strain the lemon juice into a small bowl. Cut each pear in half, peel it and cut away the core. Dip it in the lemon juice to stop it discolouring. Place it cut-side upwards in the roasting pan or dish. Arrange the pears so that they fit snugly in one layer. Put a knob of butter in the centre of each half. Drizzle the pears with the honey and pour over the leftover lemon juice and the wine.

Bake the pears in the preheated oven for about 50 minutes–1 hour, turning them halfway through. If the pears produce a lot of juice turn the heat up to 200°C (400°F) Gas 6 to concentrate the juices and form a syrup. Remove from the oven and let cool for about 20 minutes. (You can part-cook the dish for about 30 minutes a couple of hours before dinner, then finish cooking it once you sit down at table, allowing it to cool during the main course.)

Meanwhile, toast the pine nuts lightly in a frying pan, shaking them occasionally until they start to brown. Sprinkle over the caster/granulated sugar and continue to cook until the sugar melts and caramelizes. Sweeten the cream with the vanilla sugar and heat until lukewarm. Arrange 3 pear halves on each plate, trickle over about a tablespoon of warm cream and scatter over the pine nuts.

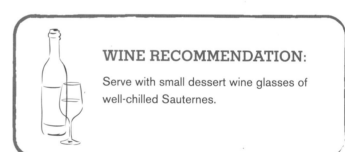

WINE RECOMMENDATION:
Serve with small dessert wine glasses of well-chilled Sauternes.

Chocolates, coffee and cognac

For a special occasion, you can serve this at the end of the meal, otherwise it makes a great substitute for a dessert. Source the best hand-made chocolates you can find, preferably made from dark chocolate, including some truffles for contrast. Brew up some real coffee – espresso for those who want it and an Americano for those who prefer a less intense brew – and serve with the best cognac or Spanish brandy you can afford.

A Celebration Tea Party

A gorgeous, girly summer tea that's perfect for any celebration: a birthday, a christening or naming day or just a special treat for your mum. There are plenty of homemade treats if you fancy a bake-in, or make a couple of the recipes and buy the rest in. Makes you wonder why we don't have tea more often...

Mini choux puffs with crab

*

Strawberry and mascarpone tartlets

*

Rose petal cupcakes

*

Pink cava and strawberry jellies

*

Raspberry and brown sugar meringues

*

Old-fashioned white wine cup

*

To Drink

There are plenty of delicious drinks to serve if you want to stick to pink – rosé Champagne (or sparkling Zinfandel if you want a wine with a touch more sweetness) and pink lemonade would be good choices. Or offer Kir Royales made with a splash of raspberry-flavoured liqueur and topped up with chilled sparkling white wine.

Mini choux puffs with crab

50 g/3 tablespoons butter, cut into cubes

75 g/½ cup strong white/all-purpose flour, sifted with ¼ teaspoon fine sea salt

2 eggs, lightly beaten

8 oz. 225 g/crabmeat

2 generous tablespoons finely chopped fresh coriander/cilantro

2 generous tablespoons mayonnaise

2 teaspoons finely chopped pickled ginger

1 tablespoon freshly squeezed lemon juice

a little grated lemon zest

sea salt and freshly ground black pepper

2 large baking sheets, lightly greased

Makes 24 puffs

Preheat the oven to 220°C (425°F) Gas 7. To make the choux puffs, melt the butter in 150 ml/⅔ cup water in a saucepan and bring to the boil. Take off the heat, add the flour and beat with a wooden spoon until the dough comes away from the side of the pan. Leave to cool for 5 minutes, then gradually beat in the eggs until you have a stiff, glossy mixture. Rinse the baking sheets with cold water, shaking off any excess so they are slightly damp (this helps the pastry rise). Using 2 teaspoons, spoon small blobs of the mixture onto the sheets, then place in the preheated oven and cook for about 18–20 minutes until brown and risen. Remove from the oven and cut a small slit in the base of each puff so that they don't collapse. Let cool on a wire rack.

Meanwhile, place the crabmeat in a bowl, taking care that you don't include any pieces of shell. Add the other ingredients and mix together lightly (you don't want to pound it into a paste). Check the seasoning adding extra lemon juice or lemon zest and salt and pepper to taste.

When the choux puffs are cold, cut them in half with a serrated knife and fill with the crab mixture. Serve immediately.

WINE RECOMMENDATION:

Serve something fizzy and pink. Try a sparkling Zinfandel or, for a special celebration lunch, a rosé Champagne.

Strawberry and mascarpone tartlets

350 g/1¾ cups plain/all-purpose flour

3 tablespoons icing/confectioners' sugar

175 g/1½ sticks butter, chilled and cut into cubes

1 large egg yolk

a pinch of salt

250 g/9 oz. mascarpone cheese

2 tablespoons caster/superfine sugar

½ teaspoon vanilla extract

1–2 tablespoons whipping cream

375 g/1 pint fresh strawberries, hulled and cut into 3

2 generous tablespoons redcurrant jelly

a 7.5-cm/3-inch pastry cutter

2 x 12-hole shallow tartlet pans

Makes 24 tartlets

To make the pastry, sift the flour and icing/confectioners' sugar into a large bowl. Cut the butter into the flour, then rub lightly between your fingertips until the mixture resembles coarse breadcrumbs. Mix the egg yolk with 3 tablespoons ice-cold water, add to the bowl, mix lightly and pull together into a ball, adding extra water if needed. Shape into a flat disc, put it in a plastic bag and refrigerate for at least half an hour.

Roll out the pastry quite thinly and stamp out rounds, re-rolling the offcuts as necessary. Gently press the rounds into the hollows in the tartlet pans. Prick the bases and chill for another half an hour. Preheat the oven to 190°C (375°F) Gas 5. Bake the pastry cases for about 15–20 minutes until lightly coloured, then set aside and cool.

Tip the mascarpone into a bowl, add the caster/superfine sugar, vanilla extract and a tablespoon of cream and beat until smooth. Add enough extra cream to give a firm but spoonable consistency. Put a generous teaspoonful of mixture into each pastry case and top with 3 strawberry pieces, arranging them so that the pointed ends meet at the top. Melt the redcurrant jelly in a pan set over gentle heat and brush it over the strawberries. You can chill the tarts briefly, but serve within 2 hours of making them.

A tea party is the perfect opportunity to serve some interesting teas and tisanes: Earl Grey or Lady Grey, for example, or fragrant Orange Pekoe. Ideally, you should make them from loose leaves in a teapot, warming the pot first and infusing them for 2–3 minutes. Encourage your guests to drink them without milk and with honey rather than sugar. Another delicious option is a tisane or infusion of fresh lemon verbena leaves (verveine to the French who are mad about it), which makes a really refreshing, slightly citrussy drink.

Rose petal cupcakes

250 g/2 sticks butter, softened

250 g/1¼ cups caster/superfine sugar

4 large eggs, beaten with 1½ teaspoons vanilla extract

250 g/2 cups self-raising flour, sifted twice

125 ml/½ cup whole milk

For the frosting:

50 g/3 tablespoons butter, softened

a few drops of pink food colouring

200 g/1½ cups icing/confectioners' sugar, sifted twice

¼ teaspoon rosewater

a small pinch of salt

2–3 tablespoons whole milk

sugar roses or other cake decorations

2 x 12-hole muffin or cake pans lined with 24 paper cake cases

Makes 24 cakes

Preheat the oven to 180°C (350°F) Gas 4. Tip the butter into a large bowl and beat with an electric hand-held whisk until smooth. Add the sugar about a third at a time and continue to beat until pale yellow and fluffy. Gradually add the beaten eggs and vanilla extract, adding a spoonful of flour with the last few additions. Fold in the remaining flour alternately with the milk, taking care not to overmix. Spoon into the paper cases and bake for about 20–25 minutes until well risen and firm to the touch. Remove from the oven and leave the cakes to cool in the pans for 5 minutes before transfering to a wire rack to cool completely.

To make the frosting, beat the butter until soft. Pour a few drops of pink food colouring onto a teaspoon (easier to control than pouring straight from the bottle), then carefully add to the butter, pouring back any excess into the bottle. Gradually add the sifted icing/confectioners' sugar 2–3 tablespoonfuls at a time. Add the rosewater, salt and enough milk to make a spreadable consistency. Spread the frosting on the tops of the cupcakes and decorate with the sugar roses. Leave to set for 2 hours before serving.

Pink cava and strawberry jellies

12 sheets of gelatine (or enough to set 1.1 litres/4½ cups of liquid)

1.1 litres/4½ cups Cava Rosado or other sparkling rosé

800 g/2 pints fresh strawberries

2–3 tablespoons caster/superfine sugar, depending on how ripe your strawberries are

90–125 ml/⅓–½ cup homemade

sugar syrup (see page 86) or shop-bought gomme

cream or vanilla ice cream, to serve

12 wine glasses or small glass serving dishes

Serves 12

Lay the gelatine in a large flat dish and sprinkle over 5–6 tablespoons cold water. Leave to soak for 3 minutes until soft. Heat the wine in a microwave or saucepan until hot but not boiling. Tip the soaked gelatine into the wine and stir to dissolve, then set aside to cool.

Rinse the strawberries, cut them into halves or quarters to give even-sized pieces and put them into a shallow bowl, sprinkle over the sugar and leave them to macerate.

Check the liquid jelly for sweetness, adding the sugar syrup to taste. Divide half the strawberries between 12 glasses or glass dishes then pour over enough jelly to cover them. Put in the fridge to chill. As soon as the jelly has set (about an hour), add the rest of the fruit and jelly. Return to the fridge to set for another 45 minutes–1 hour before serving with cream or ice cream.

• Adding a dash of strawberry-flavoured syrup or liqueur to the liquid jelly will make this even more delicious.

Raspberry and brown sugar meringues

4 large egg whites, at room temperature
150 g/¾ cup unrefined caster/superfine sugar
50 g/¼ cup light brown sugar, sifted
200 g/1½ cups frozen raspberries, unthawed

2 large, non-stick baking sheets, lightly greased with flavourless oil or lined with baking parchment

Makes 16 meringues

Preheat the oven to 150°C (300°F) Gas 2. Put the egg whites in a large, clean grease-free bowl and start to whisk them (easiest with an electric hand-held whisk). Increase the speed as they begin to froth up, moving the whisk around the bowl, until they just hold a peak (about 2–3 minutes). Gradually add the caster/superfine sugar, a teaspoonful at a time, beating the meringue well between each addition. When half the caster/superfine sugar has been incorporated, add the rest of the caster/superfine sugar a dessertspoonful at a time. Gradually add the brown sugar, then gently fold in the frozen raspberries, ensuring that they are fully coated by the meringue.

Using 2 dessertspoons, carefully spoon the meringues onto the prepared baking sheets. Place in the preheated oven and immediately reduce the heat to 140°C (275°F) Gas 1. Bake for 1¼ hours until the meringues are firm. Turn off the heat and leave the meringues to cool in the oven.

You can refrigerate the meringues for up to 3 hours, lightly covered with clingfilm/plastic wrap, before serving.

Old-fashioned white wine cup

The great virtue of white wine cups is that you can use a really basic, inexpensive dry white wine as the base. In fact, it's a positive advantage to do so. Most modern whites have too much up-front fruit flavour and alcohol for this delicate, quintessentially English summery drink.

2 x 75-cl bottles/1½ quarts very dry white wine, such as basic Vin Blanc or Muscadet, chilled
750 ml/3 cups soda water, chilled
100–125 ml//⅓–½ cup homemade sugar syrup (see page 86) or shop-bought gomme
50–100 ml/3–6 tablespoons brandy
about 20 ice cubes, to serve
orange, lemon, apple, kiwi, strawberry and cucumber slices, to serve
a few mint or borage leaves, to garnish

Makes 16 glasses

Mix the wine and soda in a jug/pitcher and add sugar syrup and brandy to taste. Prepare the fruit and add to the mix, together with ice cubes, just before serving. Serve in wine glasses, garnished with the mint or borage leaves.

A Chinese New Year Supper

The Chinese New Year is one of those annual events that captures the imagination. It is celebrated in such a colourful and joyous way and Chinese food is so delicious, quick and simple to make that we all feel inspired to have a go at it. This is a menu where you could easily buy in the dim sum and even the dessert (though this one is fun to make) but do have a go at the really delicious seafood stir-fry.

Sesame prawn toasts and other dim sum

*

Luxury seafood stir-fry

*

Stem ginger and almond ice cream, mandarin oranges and fortune cookies

*

To Drink

I've discovered that a good cold gin and tonic is exceptionally refreshing with fried dim sum such as prawn toasts and spring rolls. There are two ways to go with the wine for Chinese food – an aromatic white such as Riesling (I would recommend a young dry one from Germany or Alsace), or a fruity Bordeaux rosé, which works surprisingly well. Finish with a cup of delicate jasmine or chrysanthemum tea.

A selection of dim sum

Frankly, life is much too short to make your own dim sum, so unless you're already an expert at rolling miniature spring rolls and making featherlight steamed dumplings, order them in from your local restaurant or buy them ready-made. The exception are these simple sesame prawn toasts, which are much easier to handle than the classic Chinese deep-fried ones and can be prepared ahead and baked at the very last minute.

Sesame prawn toasts

350 g/12 oz. cooked, shelled prawns/shrimp
2–3 spring onions/scallions, trimmed and finely chopped
1 teaspoon finely grated fresh ginger or ginger paste
1 teaspoon finely grated fresh garlic or garlic paste
1½ teaspoons Vietnamese or Thai fish sauce
2 teaspoons light soy sauce
¼ teaspoon sesame oil
1 egg white
1 tablespoon ground rice
a pinch of sugar
about 5 thin slices of white bread, preferably 2–3 days old
60–75 g/about ½ cup sesame seeds
sea salt and freshly ground black pepper

2 non-stick baking sheets

Makes about 30 toasts

Put the prawns/shrimp in a food processor along with all the other ingredients, except the bread and sesame seeds, and whizz until smooth. Transfer to a bowl, cover and refrigerate for an hour or 2 for the flavours to mellow.

Preheat the oven to 230°C (450°F) Gas 8. Cut the crusts off the bread and toast lightly. Let cool, then spread each slice thickly with the prawn/shrimp paste. Cut each slice into 6. Put the sesame seeds in a shallow bowl. Press the prawn/shrimp toasts upper-side down lightly into the sesame seeds, then lay them on the baking sheets.

Bake in the preheated oven for about 5–6 minutes until the toasts are warm and the sesame seeds lightly browned. Let cool for 10 minutes before serving.

Luxury seafood stir-fry

This recipe may look complicated, but it's simply a matter of assembling the ingredients and throwing them together at the last minute in a wok.

400 g/14 oz. large prawns/shrimp
200 g/7 oz. fresh queen (small) scallops
1 tablespoon cornflour/cornstarch
sea salt and freshly ground white pepper
200 g/7 oz. broccoli, cut into small florets
3 tablespoons sunflower or light olive oil
4–6 spring onions/scallions, trimmed and thinly sliced
125 g/4½ oz. shiitake mushrooms, wiped and thinly sliced
1 garlic clove, crushed
1 knob of fresh ginger, about 2.5 cm/1 inch square, peeled and grated
½ teaspoon Sichuan pepper or crushed chillies (optional)

For the sauce:
225 ml/a scant cup light vegetable stock
freshly squeezed juice of 1 large lemon (about 3–4 tablespoons)
3–4 tablespoons rice wine, sake or fino sherry
1 tablespoon caster/superfine sugar
1 tablespoon light soy sauce
(or 1½ teaspoons dark soy sauce)
1 rounded teaspoon cornflour/cornstarch

a wok

Serves 4–6

Reserve any liquid from the prawns/shrimp and scallops. Pat them dry with paper towels and put in a large bowl. Sprinkle over the cornflour/cornstarch, season with 1 teaspoon salt and ½ teaspoon white pepper and toss thoroughly, then cover and set aside (in the fridge if you're preparing the dish more than half an hour in advance). Microwave or blanch the broccoli in boiling, salted water for 2 minutes. Drain and set aside.

To make the sauce, combine the stock with the lemon juice and 3 tablespoons of the rice wine in a jug/pitcher. Stir in the sugar and soy sauce and check the seasoning, adding more rice wine or other ingredients to taste. Mix the cornflour/cornstarch with 1 tablespoon water and put to one side.

When you're ready to cook, heat the wok, add the oil and tip in the spring onions/scallions and mushrooms. Stir-fry for 2 minutes, then add the broccoli, garlic and ginger. Stir-fry for another minute then season with Sichuan pepper, if using. Tip in the seafood, the sauce and any liquid from the prawns/shrimp and scallops and cook, stirring, until it comes to the boil (about 3 minutes). Add the cornflour/cornstarch mixture and stir until thickened. Remove from the heat and check the seasoning, adding extra salt or pepper if needed. Serve with steamed pak choi.

Stem ginger and almond ice cream

You can make this luxurious ice cream milder or stronger, depending how much ginger you use. Quantities for four people are given here as it'll fit into a standard ice cream machine. Just make the recipe twice to serve six to eight.

4–6 pieces of stem ginger, plus 3 tablespoons of syrup from the jar
150 ml/½ cup ginger wine, such as Stone's, or ginger beer, such as Reed's
1 tablespoon orange-flavoured liqueur, such as Cointreau, plus extra to serve
300 g/10½ oz. fresh (ready-made) custard/custard sauce
140 ml/a generous ½ cup whipping cream
a few drops of almond extract, to taste

fortune cookies and canned mandarin oranges, to serve

Serves 4

Chop the ginger very finely and put in a bowl. Put the syrup in a small saucepan with the ginger wine and Cointreau, bring to the boil and simmer for about 8–10 minutes until the liquid has reduced by about half. Pour over the ginger and let cool for 10 minutes.

Transfer the custard to a large bowl and stir in the ginger and syrup. Whip the cream lightly and fold it into the custard, then add the almond extract to taste. Pour the custard into an ice

cream machine and churn until firm, following the manufacturer's instructions. Or, if you don't have a machine, pour the mixture into a shallow, freezerproof container and put in the freezer, then remove after 1½ hours and whisk with an electric hand-held whisk. Repeat this freezing and whisking process 2 more times, then leave until thoroughly frozen. Store the frozen ice cream in a sealed plastic box and freeze for 24 hours.

Before serving, transfer the ice cream to the fridge for 30 minutes to make it easier to scoop. Serve with fortune cookies, or another light crisp biscuit, and mandarin oranges, drained and marinated in 2 tablespoons orange-flavoured liqueur. Do give each person 8 segments – 8 is a sacred number in China and considered to bring luck and prosperity!

Index

Picture Credits

KEY: a = above, b = below, r = right, l = left, c = centre.

Peter Cassidy
pages 1, 2, 4–8, 9c, 12–14, 36–37, 49, 50, 64, 66, 69, 71 inset, 73–75, 78 insets, 80–81, 83–84, 86–89, 92, 94 insets, 96–97, 98–99 insets, 101–104, 105 insets, 109, 111 inset, 112 insets, 115 insets, 116, 118–119 insets, 121, 123 inset, 124–128, 130–133 insets

Richard Jung
pages 9r, 38, 40–41, 43–44, 46–48, 51–55, 57–58, 61, 62, 94–95 background

William Lingwood
pages 9l, 17–18, 19 background, 21, 22–23, 25 ar, ac, al, 26 background, 29b, 31, 32–33, 35 inset, 45 inset

William Reavell
backgrounds on pages 10–11, 105–107, 110–111, 122–123

Kate Whitaker
backgrounds on pages 8–9, 12–13, 30, 34–35, 42, 70–71, 76–79, 82–83, 90–91, 98–99, 112–113, 118–119, 130–131, 137, 140–141, 142–143, 144

Alan Williams
pages 3, 16 (Berry Brothers & Rudd Ltd, London, www.bbr.com), 19 all insets, 20lc (Azienda Agricola Maculan, Breganze), 20r (Scrimaglio Winery, Italy), 24 (Maison M. Chapoutier, Châteauneuf-du-Pape, France), 26 inset, 28, 29a

Francesca Yorke
pages 25b, 30 insets